COLLINS GEM GUIDES

TREES

David More

Alastair Fitter

COLLINS
London and Glasgow

First published 1980

© Alastair Fitter and David More 1980

ISBN 0 00 458803 7

Colour reproduction by Adroit Photo-Litho Ltd, Birmingham

Filmset by Jolly & Barber Ltd, Rugby

Printed and bound by Wm Collins Sons and Co Ltd, Glasgow

Reprint 20 19 18 17 16 15 14 13

Contents

Introduction 5

Introduction

Trees and how they grow

'Tree' is one of those useful words that have no precise definition, yet are immediately understood. Most botanists envisage a plant more than 3–4m high, with a single woody stem that persists for many years, and a branched crown. The extremes are clear-cut – a well-grown beech or pine is indubitably a tree – but there is a grey area between 'trees' and 'shrubs'. Apple trees for example frequently branch at ground level, but can still produce a crown 8–10m high, whereas blackthorn is almost always a shrub, forming a dense tangled mass with no stems, but if drawn up by the shade cast by surrounding trees, it produces a single trunk and a respectable small tree.

The word tree, therefore, best describes a form of growth rather than an individual species, so this book includes species such as osier, blackthorn and alder buckthorn that are normally shrubs, but which do grow into small trees occasionally.

How, then, does a plant turn into a tree? First it must lay down wood: this is produced when *xylem*, the tissue in plant stems which transports water from roots to leaves, becomes thick-walled and toughened. Secondly, the stem must stay alive for many seasons, which means that the buds must be borne on the tip of the shoot and not at ground level, as in tall herbaceous plants, in order to survive cold winters or tropical summers.

Of course the main advantage of being a tree is to

be tall and so to get more light than surrounding plants. But basic engineering constraints require the strengthening of the base of the stem that provides support. This is brought about partly by the growth of the root system, anchoring the whole plant, and partly by the gradual thickening of the stem. Each year the whole stem from top to bottom puts on a new outer layer, so that the trunk becomes gradually thicker towards the base, and the resultant shape is in fact almost perfect from an engineer's standpoint. If you measure the height and girth of several specimens of a single species of tree you will find that there is a very close relationship maintained between them, almost throughout its life.

This continuous outward growth means that the conducting tissues are always on the edge of a tree trunk (which is why you can kill a tree by ring-barking it), and the older tissues in the centre of the trunk serve as tough supporting tissues, the channels

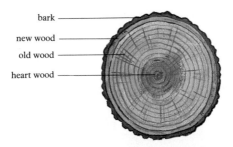

bark
new wood
old wood
heart wood

that once transported water to the leaves eventually being filled in. In temperate regions, with a cold winter during which growth ceases, this form of growth produces *annual rings*, which can be used to date a felled tree.

Some problems of being a tree

Most trees, except when planted for ornament, grow in woods and not as isolated specimens. Those magnificent trees that adorn the parks of stately homes are rather exceptional in the tree world. Few of their relations will get the chance to expand in all directions without coming up against neighbours. So, while the parkland tree grows up and out, its woodland counterpart is drawn always upward, for a tree that failed to do so would soon be overshadowed by those around it.

The shapes of trees, then, reflect their way of life. But living in woods imposes other constraints, for survival and success for a species involves shedding good seed that grows into new trees. When a seed germinates on the floor of a wood, it has little chance of growing steadily to the canopy 20, 30, perhaps

even 50 metres above it. There is too little light to allow that. Instead the seedling must wait for a tree to fall or die, letting in light, and so allowing the race for the tree-tops to begin. In a beechwood you will see many young trees a few centimetres high, but very few more than that, except where a tree has fallen some years before. There, the gap will be filled with a mass of young trees, often ash or sycamore, growing into the space. Underneath them, growing more slowly, but more tolerant of the shade they cast, will be the young beech trees, one of which will eventually become the new occupant of that particular patch of sunlight.

What to do in winter?

All plants in temperate regions have to survive winter. Annuals simply disappear and survive as seeds; herbaceous perennials keep their buds near or in the ground, where they can be better protected. But a tree must have its buds high up, where the battle for light is taking place. This is why deciduous trees lose their leaves each autumn, leaving the frost-resistant buds on the high branches, to grow a new crop of leaves each spring. Deciduousness does involve an enormous waste of resources – all those dead leaves – but it means that the leaves themselves need not be frost-resistant and so can be much more efficient. In arctic regions the forests are of evergreen trees whose leaves need to be frost resistant. This makes them less efficient but enables them to survive all year round.

Why be a tree?

The chief advantage in being a tree is the amount of light it gets simply by being bigger than other plants. The disadvantage of being a tree is that it must survive in one place for a long time. If fires, land-slides, or hurricanes are regular events, the tree may die without ever having reproduced. In fact in most temperate regions the natural environment does favour trees in most places, and human activity is the major factor militating against them. For example it is thought that in about 4000 BC almost the whole of Britain was covered by woodland, and it has mostly been cleared by men using axes or fire.

Woodlands

Some trees grow faster than others. The typical forest trees, such as oak and beech, are rather slow-growing compared to such trees as birch and alder. These can almost be thought of as tree 'weeds', for they have a surprising amount in common with garden weeds. They produce huge numbers of very small seeds, sometimes with wings, which travel considerable distances, and are likely to fall in a place where no trees are growing. Once there they grow rapidly and begin to produce new seeds when perhaps as little as five years old, to start the cycle off again.

In contrast oak trees produce many fewer seeds, but their acorns contain lots of food for the developing seedling, giving it a good start in life, particularly if it finds itself under a canopy of other trees. On the other hand an acorn is not well adapted to travelling long distances – unless a jay or a squirrel carries it off and buries it. Once established the seedling grows rather slowly and may not produce seed until it is 20 or 30 years old.

Woods tend therefore to be composed of these longer-lived trees, of which the best example is oak. Over most of Britain and much of Europe the vegetation that would occur in the absence of human interference is oakwood of some sort, although several different species of oak are involved. In Britain the other important forest-forming trees are beech, which grows best on the dry chalk hills and sands of southern England; Scots pine which once formed extensive forests in Scotland; ash which is characteristic of steep limestone valleys in northern and western England; and alder which grows in wet valleys and fens.

Birch is also now a common woodland tree, but it owes its prominence to man, for it is normally a coloniser of areas that have been cleared and then abandoned, such as heaths and moors.

There are of course many other trees, each with its own *niche*, but few of them really form woods. Some

are common in woods, usually as rather isolated individuals, while others are introduced and are found either in plantations or in parks and gardens.

Man and woodlands

In Britain there are a few areas that have been woodland throughout all or most of their history – survivors of the ancient forests that once covered the country. They have a richer flora and fauna and, in particular, more of the unusual trees and shrubs (such as wild service tree) than the more recent plantations.

To our ancestors the wood was an essential part of the rural economy. It provided two things: timber for houses, and wood for fuel and minor constructions such as the making of hurdles. In order to produce these efficiently the coppicing system, once so characteristic of lowland England, was evolved.

A well-managed coppice contains a number of tall 'standard' trees, well-spaced and not taking much

light away from the plants underneath; and a shrub layer which is regularly cut back to leave stumps which then produce long shoots. The standards provide the timber and the coppiced shrubs offer wood. As standards are felled so occasional saplings are allowed to grow through to replace them. In those few woods that are still coppiced in this traditional pattern, the shrub layer consists of a mosaic, in all stages of regrowth from the recently cut back to those parts about to be cut; this continual opening up of the ground to sunlight allows woodland plants such as primroses to flourish.

Identifying trees

The identification of plants can seem a formidable task when you are just beginning, and the feats of those who wander around murmuring '*Salix fragilis* clearly' or '*Pseudotsuga menziesii* I think' may be a little unnerving. They achieve this, however, not by magic but by a process of quick categorization and elimination, and the basic rules of the game are quite easy to learn. If a botanist has no idea what a particular plant is, he uses a key to identify it with. Proper botanical keys have lists of paired questions, and one for this book might start off with:

1 Leaves small and scale-like or needle-like
Gymnosperms (Conifers) 2

1a Leaves large and/or flat, often transparent
Angiosperms (Broad-leaved trees) 50

If your tree had needles you would have a conifer and you would go to question 2, which would ask you about some other diagnostic feature. If, in contrast, statement **1a** seemed more appropriate then you would have a broad-leaved tree and would skip the next 48 questions and move on to question 50.

In practice everyone can tell a pine tree from an oak, which is really all this distinction amounts to, but in doing so you have narrowed the choice of which your unknown one might be, by a very considerable margin. Becoming more skilled at identification is simply a matter of carrying a few more of these distinctions in your head, so that when you start using the book, you are roughly in the right area and have to choose from only a few possibilities.

First of all, though, you need to know what to look out for. Leaves are often good characters, in particular their size, shape, colour and the length of the stalk, but the most reliable guides are the flowers and fruit. You will soon notice that most conifers have cones rather than proper flowers, and that broad-leaved trees are roughly divided into those, such as willows, poplars, oaks, and birches, that bear catkins, and those, for example apples and plums, that have what is easily recognized as a flower, large and with conspicuous petals. Pages 26–7 are a quick pictorial guide to the cones you may encounter, and pages 80–1 perform the same service for catkins.

In winter, unless you are dealing with an evergreen tree, neither leaves nor flowers are available and you will have to rely on bark and twig characters. The key on pp. 20–5 is intended to help you here. Instead of a series of questions for you to work your way through, it consists of a number of boxes, each of which represents a particular combination of bark type and colour, obtained by working along the rows, and bud size and colour, found by working down the columns. So if your leafless tree has smooth grey bark and large green buds it must be either fig, elder, or whitebeam, and the correct answer is easily checked by turning to the relevant plates. This sort of key is easy to use because it sets out in print the mental processes that an experienced botanist is rapidly and subconsciously going through.

Similarly you may often come across trees in full leaf that have neither flowers nor fruit and the box-key on pp. 16–19 will help you identify these. Once you have decided upon leaf shape and colour, you will be left with a short-list of from one to a dozen or so species to choose from. In addition, scattered through the text are some special keys to particularly difficult groups.

Mature Foliage

	Green	Dark Green
Scales	Savin 42, Western Red Cedar 44, Coast Redwood 46	Cypresses 34–8, Phoenician Juniper 42
Needles	Giant Fir 54, Douglas Fir 58, Sitka Spruce 62, European Larch 64, Hybrid Larch 64, Deodar 66, Monterey Pine 76	Yew 30, Coast Redwood 46, Silver Fir 54, Hemlocks 60, Norway Spruce 62, Lebanon and Atlas Cedar 68, Mountain 72, Austrian 74, Shore 74, Arolla 78, and Weymouth 78 Pine
Narrow leaves	Crack and Hoary Willow 82, Osier 90, Nettle Tree 138, Wild Pear 148, Peach 170, Spindle-tree 202	Bay and Almond Willow 88, Sweet Chestnut 114, Almond 168, Strawberry Tree 220, Box 204
Oval leaves	Black Poplars 96, Silver Birch 104, Apples 152, Common Lime 212, Indian Bean Tree 228	Monkey Puzzle 32, Aspen 94, Western Balsam Poplar 98, European Hop-hornbeam 108, Cultivated Apple 132
Elliptical leaves	English, Small-leaved and Fluttering Elm 134, White Mulberry 140, Cultivated Apple 152, Blackthorn 172, Cherries 166–80, Portugal Laurel 180, Oranges 188, Lemon 188, Broad-leaved Spindle-tree 202, Cornelian Cherry 216	Hornbeam 108, Beech 112, Holm 128, Cork 130 and Holly 130 Oaks, Wych 132, Dutch 132 and English 134 Elm, Black Mulberry 140, Common Pear 148, Swedish and Broad-leaved Whitebeams 158, Blackthorn 172, Plums 174, Bird Cherry 178, Box 204, Rhododendron 218, Strawberry Tree 220

Yellow-Green	Blue- and Grey-Green	Grey
Leyland 36 and Monterey 38 Cypress, White Cedar 44	Leyland Cypress 36, Wellingtonia 48	Leyland Cypress 36
Japanese Red Cedar 50, Swamp Cypress 52, Dawn Redwood 52, Giant Fir 54, Deodar 66, Shore Pine 74	Swamp Cypress 52, Dawn Redwood 52, Noble Fir 56, Douglas Fir 58, Japanese and Hybrid Larch 64, Cedars 68, Stone 70, Maritime 70, Scots 72, Austrian 74, and Monterey 76 Pine	Firs (*Abies*) 54–8, Hemlocks 60
Weeping Willow 84, Almond 168, Peach 170	White 82 and Grey 86 Willow, Wild Pear 148, Medlar 162, Gums 214, Olive 224	Bay 88, Grey 86 and Crack 82 Willow, Sallow 86, Willow-leaved Pear 148, Gums 214
Balsam Poplars 98, Cultivated Apple 152, Small-leaved Lime 210, Indian Bean Tree 228	Aspen 94	
Weeping Willow 84, Common Pear 148, Whitebeam 158, Snowy Mespil 160, Wild Cherry 176, Cherry Laurel 180, Magnolias 144	Grey Alder 106, Round-leaved Oak 128, Whitebeam 158, Cornelian Cherry 216, Medlar 162	Holm 128 and Cork 130 Oak, Whitebeams 158

	Green	**Dark Green**
Rounded leaves	Downy Birch 104, Green Alder 106, Wild Pear 148, Apricot 170, Buckthorns 206, Common Lime 212	Alder 106, Hazel 110, Large-leaved Lime 212, Judas Tree 182, Holly 200
Lobed leaves	English 118, Pin 122, and Pyrenean 124 Oak, Tulip Tree 144, London Plane 146, Hawthorns 164	English 118, Durmast 120, Red 122, and Turkey 124 Oaks, Holly 200
Pinnate leaves	Rowan 154, Pagoda Tree 184, Tree of Heaven 190, Elder 230, Canary Palm 232	Black Walnut 102, Locust Tree 184, Ashes 222, Pagoda Tree 184
Trefoil leaves	Hawthorns 164, Montpelier Maple 194, London Plane 146	Fig 142, Italian Maple 196
Forked leaves	Tulip Tree 144	Ginkgo 28
Palmate leaves	London Plane 146, Wild Service Tree 156, Hawthorn 164, Norway 192 and Field 194 Maple, Horse Chestnut 198, Sycamore 196	Fig 142, Field 194 and Italian 196 Maple, Sycamore 196, Horse Chestnut 198

Yellow-Green	Blue- and Grey-Green	Grey
Buckthorns 206, Judas Tree 182	Grey Poplar 92	Gums 214
Pin Oak 122	Downy Oak 126	Pyrenean Oak 124
Common Walnut 102, True Service Tree 154, Locust Tree 184, Common Ash 222, Mimosa 186	Locust Tree 184, Date Palm 232	
Laburnums 182	Laburnums 182	
Ginkgo 28		
London Plane 146, Norway Maple 192	White and Grey Poplar 92	

Key to Broad-leaved Trees in Winter

Small (less than 5mm)

BARKS \ BUDS	Brown and Grey	Red and Orange-Brown	Green and Green-Brown
Smooth	Weeping Willow 84, Cornelian Cherry 216		Mimosa 186, Cornelian Cherry 216
Flaking or Peeling	Almond Willow 88, Hawthorns 164, Italian Maple 196, Cornelian Cherry 216	Dawn Redwood 52, Crab Apple 152, Strawberry Tree 220	Birches 104, Dawn Redwood 52, Cornelian Cherry 216
Cracked or Scarred	Hawthorns 164, Italian Maple 196	Wild Pear 148, Crab Apple 152, Box 204	Birches 40
Ridged	Pagoda Tree 184	Judas Tree 182, Indian Bean Tree 228	

Brown, Red or Orange-Brown

Small (less than 5mm)

BARKS \ BUDS	Brown and Grey	Red and Orange-Brown	Green and Green-Brown
Smooth	Red Oak 122, Nettle Tree 138, Snowy Mespil 160, Blackthorn 172	Sallow 86, Blackthorn 172, Tree of Heaven 190	Cherry Laurel 180, Holly 200, Spindle-tree 202
Flaking or Peeling	Bird and St Lucie's Cherry 178, Hawthorns 164,	Fluttering Elm 134, Field Maple 194	Birches 40, Wild Service Tree 156
Cracked or Scarred	Bay 88, and Crack 82 Willow, Italian Maple 196, Birches 104	Willow-leaved Pear 150, Field and Montpelier Maple 194	Birches 40, Wild Service Tree 156
Ridged	White and Crack Willow 82, Locust Tree 184	Crack Willow 82, Small-leaved Elm 184, Field Maple 194	Hop-hornbeam 108

White, Grey or Grey-Brown

Key to Broad-leaved Trees in Winter

Medium 5–15mm

BARKS \ BUDS	Grey, Grey-Brown and Black	Brown	Red and Orange-Brown	Green and Green-Brown
Smooth	Cork Oak 130, Scotch Laburnum 182	Wild Plum 174, Peach 190, Alder Buckthorn 208	Wild Plum 174	Alder Buckthorn 208
Flaking or Peeling	Laburnum 182, Italian Maple 196	Larch 64, Buckthorn 206	Dutch Elm 132, London Plane 146, Apple 152, Hawthorns 164, Wild Cherry 176	Laburnum 182
Cracked or Scarred		English Elm 134, Cherry-plum 174	Mulberries 140, Crab Apple 152	Alder 106, True Service Tree 154
Ridged		Honey-locust 184	Black Poplar 96, White Mulberry 140	True Service Tree 154

Brown, Red or Orange-Brown

22

White, Grey or Grey-Brown

BARKS \ BUDS	Grey, Grey-Brown and Black	Brown	Red and Orange-Brown	Green and Green-Brown
Smooth	Magnolias 144, Ashes 222	Aspen 94, Hazel 110, English Oak 118, Wild Plum 174, Cherry 196	Sallow 86, Grey and Green Alder 106, Swedish Whitebeam 158, Japanese Cherries 170, Norway Maple 192	Hornbeam 108, Hazel 110, Norway Maple 192, Sycamore 196
Flaking or Peeling	Magnolias 144, London Plane 146	Hazel 110, Medlar 162	London Plane 146, Apple 152, Medlar 162, Hawthorn 164, Japanese Cherries 170	Hazel 110, Sycamore 196
Cracked or Scarred		Pyrenean Oak 124, Almond 168	Tulip Tree 144, Crab Apple 152, Japanese Cherries 170, Small-leaved Lime, 212	Alder 106, True Service Tree 154
Ridged	Cork Oak 130, Wych Elm 132, Ashes 222	Maidenhair Tree 28, Turkey Oak 124	White and Grey Poplar 92, Sweet Chestnut 114, Small 212, and Large-leaved Lime 210	Hornbeam 108, True Service Tree 154

23

Key to Broad-leaved Trees in Winter

Large (more than 15mm)

BUDS / BARKS	Brown, Grey and Black	Red and Orange-Brown	Green
Smooth			Rhododendron 218
Flaking or Peeling		Horse Chestnut 198	Larch 64
Cracked or Scarred		Horse Chestnut 198	
Ridged	Elder 230	Black Walnut 102, Elder 230	

Brown, Red or Orange-Brown

Large (more than 15mm)

BARKS \ BUDS	Brown, Grey and Black	Red and Orange-Brown	Green
Smooth	Beech 112, Rowan 154, Ashes 222	Poplar 92, Balsam Poplars 98	Fig 142, Whitebeam 158. Elder 230
Flaking or Peeling		Horse Chestnut 198	
Cracked or Scarred	Beech 112	Balm of Gilead 98, Downy Oak 126. Horse Chestnut 198	
Ridged	English Oak 118, Ashes 222	Walnut 102, English 118, Durmast 120 and Downy 126 Oak, Common Lime 210	Elder 230

White, Grey or Grey-Brown

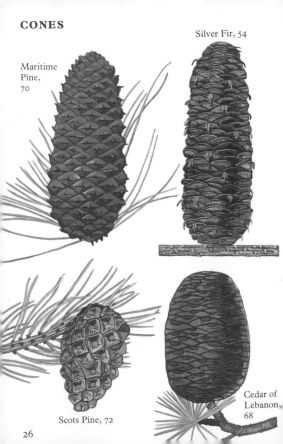

Maritime
Pine,
70

Silver Fir, 54

Scots Pine, 72

Cedar of
Lebanon,
68

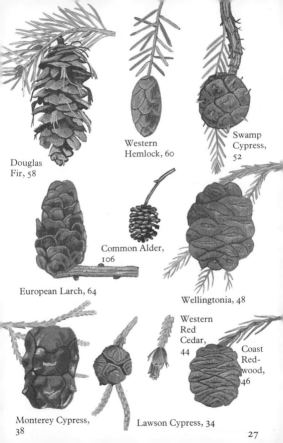

Douglas Fir, 58

Western Hemlock, 60

Swamp Cypress, 52

European Larch, 64

Common Alder, 106

Wellingtonia, 48

Western Red Cedar, 44

Coast Redwood, 46

Monterey Cypress, 38

Lawson Cypress, 34

27

MAIDENHAIR TREE *Ginkgo biloba*

This extraordinary primitive tree, which has no known living relatives, was introduced from China and is now commonly planted in parks and gardens, except in the north. Maidenhair Tree has a fossil record stretching back 200 million years and was once widespread throughout the northern hemisphere. Its leaves (**3**) are unmistakable, rather like a maidenhair fern (hence the name), fan-shaped, split down the middle, and with veins that fork equally. Unlike most gymnosperms it is deciduous, the leaves falling (**5**) late to reveal green twigs, later turning brown, with small reddish buds (**2**). The leaves are borne on stout short shoots, which give it something of the appearance of a fruit tree in winter. Flowers are rare and on separate trees, the male in yellow catkins, the female globular on short stalks. Fruit green, turning yellow-brown and foul-smelling. Old trees can reach 30m (**4**) with greyish, deeply ridged bark (**1**), but they are slow-growing and typical specimens are 10–15m, with a rather narrow, conical crown.

1

COMMON YEW   *Taxus baccata*

Yew is very long lived (to 2,000 years) and
makes a massive but usually squat tree (**5**)
with dark green, evergreen, flattened needles
which are poisonous to cattle. The trunk is
often fluted, owing to the coalescence of
shoots which are repeatedly produced from
its base, and the bark is reddish and flaking
(**1**). The male (**2**) and female flowers (**3**),
borne on separate trees, are inconspicuous,
but the male trees will release clouds of pollen
if knocked in early spring. The poisonous
fruit (**4**) is pinkish-red, cup-shaped and resembles a berry, but it is actually termed an
aril as it does not enclose the seed which lies at
the base of the cup. Yew is widespread in
central Europe, extending to Norway, western Scotland and Ireland; in England it is
characteristically found on the chalk downs in
the south or on limestone hills in the north
and west.

Irish Yew (**6**) or golden forms are often
planted in gardens and yew trees are a familiar sight in churchyards, where the oldest
specimens may pre-date the foundations of
the church as yew had important pre-
Christian religious significance.

1

3

4

5

6

MONKEY PUZZLE or CHILE PINE
Araucaria araucaria

This quite unmistakable evergreen tree is most commonly found in suburban gardens. Typical examples have a long, straight trunk, capped by whorls of spreading branches (**5**), but better-developed specimens may have more domed crowns. The rough bark is grey or brown and shows annual growth rings (**1**). The twigs are made of armour-like plates each of which produces a tough, dark green, spiny leaf (**4**) and these almost completely hide the stem. Male flowers (**3**) are large and cluster at the tips of stems; female flowers (**2**) appear on the same trees but take two years to ripen into a large spiny fruit (**6**). Monkey Puzzle was introduced from South America in the late eighteenth century, and is the only member of this genus (named after a tribe of South American Indians) grown on any scale in Britain.

1

young tree

2

3

4

5

6

LAWSON CYPRESS
Chamaecyparis lawsoniana

This striking, tall evergreen (**6**) from the mountains of western North America is now widely planted for both commercial and amenity purposes. Open-grown plants can reach 40m in Britain and have narrow, conical crowns with drooping tips and branches all the way down to the ground. The bark is usually fissured or cracked (**1**). The twigs (**2**) are reddish, clothed with scale leaves and smell of parsley when crushed. Red male flowers (**3**) and blue-grey female flowers (**4**) are produced at the tips of the twigs in April. Unlike the true cypresses, the cones (**5**) mature in the same year; they are less than 1cm long and shed winged seeds. Lawson Cypress is a fast-growing, hardy tree which is widely planted and has many varieties.

Nootka Cypress *C. nootkatensis* is another North American species but one that is much less common than Lawson Cypress, from which it differs in its smooth conical crown (**9**) yellow male flowers (**7**) and its slower-maturing fruit (**8**) which is bluer, slightly larger and more spiny. The flowers and fruit also distinguish it from the similar Leyland Cypress, p. 36.

1

LEYLAND CYPRESS
× *Cupressocyparis leylandii*

Although now probably the most widely planted garden evergreen, Leyland Cypress is a botanical rarity. It is a hybrid between two genera, *Cupressus* and *Chamaecyparis*, the true and false cypresses respectively, and the various types represent crosses between different pairs of species. Leyland Cypress is a tall, narrow, fast-growing and hardy tree (**6**) although, because of the phenomenal rate at which it is being planted, it is most likely to be seen as a young specimen or even as a hedge (**8**). The bark (**1**) is sometimes reddish and slightly fissured and the leaves clothing the rather stiff shoots are scale-like, yellow-green, green, blue-green or greyish. The different leaf colours distinguish the various clones sold commercially, including grey (**5**), green (**4**) and blue (**7**) forms. Twigs are either flattened or branching in all planes. Unusually, for a hybrid between two genera, Leyland Cypress produces both male (**2**) and female flowers, the female cones (**3**) being about 2cm long, intermediate between the true and false cypresses.

1

2

3

4

5

6

7

8

MONTEREY CYPRESS
Cupressus macrocarpa

True cypresses, *Cupressus*, are distinguished from the false and hybrid cypresses (p. 36) by their larger, slow-to-mature cones and their spiky-looking twigs. Monterey Cypress is a massive, spreading tree reaching 35m and resembling a cedar (7). It has brown, ridged bark (1) and yellowish lemon-scented scale-leaves, tightly clothing the twigs (4). The small male flowers (5) are yellow and further up the twigs than the female. The purple-brown cones (6), up to 4cm across, have 7–14 scales, each with a central boss. A very fast-growing (10), salt-resistant tree from California that is widely planted.

Italian Cypress *C. sempervirens* is a native of the Aegean, but planted all over the Mediterranean and occasionally as far north as Scotland. In cultivation characteristically pencil-shaped, but wild plants may be spreading. Its minute, dark green scale-leaves (8) are scentless when crushed and it has rounder, yellow-grey cones (9) and darker bark (2).

Smooth Arizona Cypress *C. glabra* is intermediate in shape, with purple-brown bark (3) flaking to red or yellow. This widely-planted and very hardy tree has blue-grey leaves (11) and purple-brown cones (12) which stay on the tree when ripe.

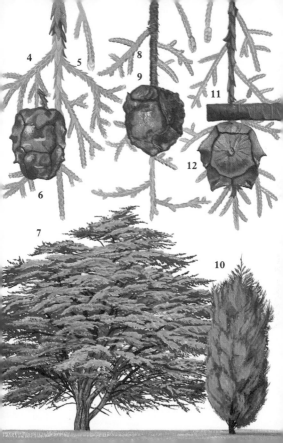

COMMON JUNIPER
Juniperus communis

This is the most widespread tree or shrub in Europe and one of the most variable. It ranges from the dwarf subspecies *nana* (**4**), to both columnar, even pencil-shaped forms (var. *hibernica* (**3**)) and broad and spreading forms (**5**). Usually 2–3m high, it rarely grows as high as 15m. It has flattened, sharp needles (**1**) in whorls of three, grey-green to yellow-green with a broad grey band on the inner side. Male and female flowers are produced on separate trees: the less numerous males in small yellow cones (**1**), the female in green cones which gradually ripen to become fleshy blue-black berries (**2**) 5–9mm across, over two or three years. These berries give gin its distinctive flavour. Juniper grows in many habitats including dry mountainsides, chalk downs, and in pinewoods, but rarely in shade.

Prickly Juniper *J. oxycedrus* tends to be larger than Common Juniper and is found only in southern Europe. It can be identified by the two grey stripes on the inside of the leaves (**6**) and its large berries which measure up to 15mm and are reddish or purple-brown when ripe (**6**).

PHOENICIAN JUNIPER
Juniperus phoenicea

A small tree or shrub (**2**) which differs from Common Juniper in having only scale leaves – making it look rather like a cypress – though young plants have needles too. The scales cling closely to the stem (**1**) and have a narrow papery border; the needles on young plants have two grey bands on each side. Male and female cones grow on the same plant, the female ripening from dark green to a rich red-brown berry 8–14mm across. It grows characteristically on dry, often stony hillsides and on sand dunes near the Mediterranean.

Savin *J. sabina* is usually only a shrub. The immature needles grow in pairs, and the mature scales are unbordered and foul-smelling when crushed. Cones measure only 4–6mm and ripen in one year to a purplish black (**3**). It grows mainly in the mountains of central Europe.

Pencil Cedar *J. virginiana* can grow up to 30m in height (**5**). The twigs are loosely clothed with scale leaves and smell oily when crushed; needles sometimes survive on adult trees. The fruits are blue-grey when young (**4**), but brownish-violet when ripe. A native of North America, Pencil Cedar is widely planted, sometimes for timber.

WESTERN RED CEDAR
Thuja plicata

Western Red Cedar is not a true cedar but is
the 'cedar' of the timber trade. It is a tall, nar-
rowly conical, well-clothed tree (**5**), capable
of 65m, but only 40m in Britain, and usually
unbranched, though sometimes layering at
the base to form new trunks, with dark purplish, ridged bark (**1**). Its leading shoot remains
upright, unlike Lawson Cypress (p. 34). The
scale-leaves (**3**) are bright-green, white-
streaked underneath (**4**), and very aromatic.
Female and male flowers are found on one
tree, the former conical, floppy-looking,
10–15mm, eventually rather spiny (**2**). It is
often planted in gardens in a form with
golden-striped foliage, but it is also a valuable
and fast-growing timber tree, though native
in North America.

White Cedar, *T. occidentalis*, is the most
commonly planted of the other *Thuja* species.
It has a more ragged crown, brighter, more
flaking bark, and duller, yellowish foliage. Its
scale-leaves (**6**) are not white-streaked and
less strongly-scented; cones yellow, more
oblong. Often planted as a yellow-leaved
variety.

1

COAST REDWOOD
Sequoia sempervirens

In its native forests of the coastal hills of
western North America, Coast Redwoods
grow to over 100m: the world's tallest surviving tree is a *Sequoia* 112m high. Its characteristic oblong, rather open and untidy crown (**2**)
sits on a tall, unbranched, though often
suckering trunk, thickly clad in soft, spongy,
flaking, red-brown bark (**1**). The stems are
clothed in narrow, rather twisted scale-leaves
(**4**), but bear twigs with opposite ranks of stiff,
dark-green, pointed linear leaves (**3**), each
with a pair of white bands underneath. The
male cones (**6**) are yellow, on the ends of
twigs, carried throughout the winter and
ripening in February; female cones 20–25cm
long, green and bristly, turning brown (**5**) and
with widely separated scales. A very impressive and fast-growing tree, typically
reaching 30–40m in Britain so far in the 130
years since it was introduced; most mature
wild trees are 500–1000 years old.

1

Coast Redwood   Wellingtonia

2

3

4

5

6

WELLINGTONIA
Sequoiadendron giganteum

Wellingtonia is a shorter but more massive tree than Coast Redwood, with a neater more conical crown and lower branches that characteristically droop then turn upwards at the tip (**2**). Its foliage is, however, strikingly different, being composed entirely of dull green or grey-green scale leaves (**3**), tightly pressed against the stem when young, but more bristly in appearance on older branches. The male cones are densely clustered on the youngest shoot tips and ripen in early spring; the female cones are egg-shaped and measure 5–8cm in length (**4**). The trunk is massive and the bark (**1**) very similar to that of Coast Redwood, but brighter in young trees; it is characteristically excavated by treecreepers for roost sites. In California trunks 25m in girth have been measured, though these are probably over 3,000 years old, while in Britain the trees have grown to 7–8m in girth over 120 years. Wellingtonia is very commonly planted in parks, at road junctions and by ambitious gardeners.

1

JAPANESE RED CEDAR
Cryptomeria japonica

This attractive Japanese tree has a tall, narrow, rounded, and rather irregular crown, formed of short rising branches, giving the appearance of a conical green cumulus cloud (**2**). It reaches 30–40m in Britain, about 50m in Japan, and has red-brown bark (**1**), darkening slowly with age and peeling in long shreds. In general appearance the foliage resembles Wellingtonia but it is brighter green and spiky looking. The leaves are hard, rather fleshy needles, arranged in five ranks around the twigs and shortest at the tips (**3**). The female cones (**4**) are spherical, 2–3cm in diameter and each scale has several short spines. Japanese Red Cedar is not, of course, a true cedar but a primitive relative of Wellingtonia and Coast Redwood. It grows in both China and Japan, and trees of Chinese origin have a less bushy crown and longer leaves (**5**). In gardens the most commonly encountered cultivar is 'Elegans' which is much slower growing and has a purplish tinge to the foliage.

1

2

3

4

5

SWAMP CYPRESS *Taxodium distichum*
An unmistakable tree (**7**) with a sharply narrowing, buttressed trunk, often surrounded by curious pegs or knees called pneumatophores (**8**) rising from the ground. It is a native of south-eastern North America, in swamps where the knees are thought to help the roots breathe. The bark is reddish (**1**) and fibrous as in Coast Redwood, but thinner and peeling in strips. The flat linear leaves (**5**) are grey-striped underneath and clear apple-green when young; they are arranged in two alternating ranks along side shoots which are also alternately placed. Both these shoots and the leaves are shed in the autumn (**4**). The male flowers (**3**) are produced in lumpy catkins which lengthen during the winter until they reach maturity in April. The small, rounded female cones (**6**) are purplish-brown when ripe. Swamp Cypress is often planted by water.

1

2

Dawn Redwood *Metasequoia glyptostroboides* is a commonly planted deciduous tree, resembling a small Swamp Cypress, but with larger, paler leaves (**9**) set opposite each other on oppositely-placed side shoots, and more brightly coloured bark (**2**). It was only known as a fossil until 1948 when discovered growing wild in south-west China.

3

4

5

6

7

8

9

COMMON SILVER FIR *Abies alba*

Although not native to Britain, this is the commonest European silver fir and grows in all the central European mountains and in one area of northern France. It is now rarely planted but it was introduced early and so is widespread. It is an imposing and attractive tree (**2**) up to 50m in height, with repeated whorls of branches, making a rather ragged oblong crown which often dies back at the tip. The bark (**1**) is smooth and grey at first but browns and cracks with age. The flat leaves, rounded at the tip, are dark green above (**3**) and have a distinct midrib and two white bands underneath (**4**); they leave the shoot both horizontally and slanting upwards, but not vertically, so leaving a distinct parting (**3**). The small male flowers are borne all over the tree, but the cylindrical female cones (**5**) stand 10–20cm upright on the higher branches only; they are orange-brown when mature and tightly closed until disintegrating to shed seed.

1

Giant Fir *A. grandis* is now more often planted because of its rapid growth. The shiny, aromatic leaves vary in length and project more or less horizontally (**6**). The cones (**7**) are smaller (5–10cm), more rounded and red-brown.

2

3

4

5

6

7

NOBLE FIR   *Abies procera*

Like the Giant Fir, Noble Fir is an introduction from North America which is widely
planted in western Britain. Initially the crown
is neatly conical but the tree matures to produce a massive almost straight-sided crown
(**2**). The bark (**1**) is characteristically smooth
and only slightly cracked even in old trees.
The leaves are strikingly blue-grey and
stubby, parting beneath the twig and arched
up around it, giving a toothbrush effect (**3**).
The male flowers are bright red when mature
and the massive cones (20–25cm) are cylindrical with prominently protruding bracts
arranged around it in spirals (**4**). Noble Fir is
unmistakable with its combination of massive, upright cones and blue-grey, rather
bristly-looking foliage.

Spanish Fir *A. pinsapo* is a curious short-
needled fir that grows as a native only in a few
small woods on the hills around Ronda in
south Spain. Occasionally planted in gardens,
it is distinguished by its dark bark, very short
needles, and much shorter cones.

1

DOUGLAS FIR *Pseudotsuga menziesii*

A tall, elegant conifer providing some of the tallest trees in Britain (there are several over 50m) and holding the world height record of 127m for a tree felled in British Columbia in 1895. Vigorous trees produce a narrow open crown with horizontal branches (**2**) but more compact stunted trees are often seen. The dark purple-brown bark (**1**) is thick and has huge fissures. The aromatic leaves are very variable in colour but are usually dull and have two white stripes beneath; they leave the shoot in all directions (**3**). The distinctive cones (**4**) up to 8cm long, hang from the ends of branches and have long three-toothed bracts hiding the cone scales. Douglas Fir is very widely planted and an extremely valuable timber tree. It is most likely to be confused with Silver Fir but it has more prominent reddish-brown, pointed buds, and the pendulous cones and the thick fissured bark are quite distinctive.

1

seed

WESTERN HEMLOCK
Tsuga heterophylla

An elegant, conical tree (**7**) with a very characteristic drooping leading shoot and branches which point slightly upwards. Old trees lose their regular outline and the bark which is smooth and flaking when young develops narrow fissures (**1**). The leaves have a curiously irregular look as they occur in three different sizes and leave the shoot at all angles (**4** and **5**); they have rounded tips and two white bands underneath (**4**). The male cones (**3**) are conspicuously bright red-purple and turn white in spring, but the females (**6**) ripen to small (2–3cm), greenish-brown, neatly egg-shaped cones. This hemlock is one of several western North American trees which are now widely planted in western Europe for timber; it is particularly valuable as it can withstand deeper shade than most conifers and so can be planted under existing trees.

Eastern Hemlock *T. canadensis* is the East Coast equivalent of Western Hemlock and so is less well suited to the European climate. It has a more untidy crown, coarsely fissured bark (**2**), smaller cones (**8**) and leaves with narrower white bands (**9**), arranged in two neat rows along the shoots. It is rarely used for forestry and mainly planted for ornament.

3

4

5

6

7

8

9

NORWAY SPRUCE *Picea abies*

This is the true Christmas tree and the native European spruce, although introduced into Britain. Its crown is very regular and conical with more-or-less level branches often turned up at the tips (**5**). The stiff, sharp needles are pale green when first produced but soon turn a deep dark green; they lie half-flattened against the stem and except for a small gap on the under side cover the stem densely (**2**). When they fall they leave a characteristic 'peg' (**4**). The bark (**1**) usually has a slight reddish tinge and is thin, rough and cracked. Spruce cones (**3**) are up to 18cms long, cylindrical and always hang downwards. Norway Spruce forms huge natural forests in the European mountains and is widely planted for timber and Christmas sales (**6**).

Sitka Spruce *P. sitchensis* is a native of western North America that flourishes in western Europe in areas of high rainfall, reaching 50m, and is now probably the commonest tree in Britain. It is the fastest growing tree on wet, peaty, upland soils and so has been planted in millions for forestry; in addition spontaneous seedlings often occur. It is distinguished by its flattened, bluish, even sharper needles (**7**) and its much smaller, more rounded, pale brown cones.

1

2

3

4

5

6

7

EUROPEAN LARCH   *Larix decidua*

Larches are much the commonest winter-bare conifers – the others are Dawn Redwood and Swamp Cypress – and are easily distinguished by their knobbly twigs (**1**). European Larch is an elegant tree (**3**) with down-sweeping branches turning upwards (sometimes vertically) at the tips; it can reach 45m in cultivation but 30–35m is more usual in the wild. The bark (**2**) is grey or brown, breaking into long fissures. The limp, bright-green needles are borne in neat tufts (**4**) from late March to October, when they fall golden-brown, on special 'short shoots' (the knobs) which never elongate. Male (**6**) and female (**7**) cones are often borne on the same twig: the females are feathery and purplish-red; the males are less than 1cm long, bright yellow with a purplish ring round the base, and shedding pollen in April. The mature cone (**5**) is egg-shaped, smooth, less than 4cm long and will often remain on the tree for years.

Japanese Larch *L. kaempferi* has dull orange-brown (not yellowish) twigs, flatter, greyer needles, and cones (**8**) with outward-pointing scales. It is a native of Japan and like the hybrid between these, Hybrid Larch *L. × eurolepis* which is intermediate in most characters (**9**), is planted more than *L. decidua* because of its very rapid growth rate.

1

2

3

4

5

6

7

8

9

DEODAR *Cedrus deodara*

Cedars are massive evergreen trees with tufts of needles borne on special 'short shoots', as in the larches. Deodar is an attractive, conical tree (**2**) with a drooping main shoot and lower branches often sweeping down to ground level, obscuring the dark, smooth or finely cracked trunk (**1**). Its needles are longer than those of other cedars (3–4cm) and are initially borne in a widely-spaced spiral on young twigs, and then in tufts (**3**). The long, cylindrical, slightly curved male cones are conspicuously purple when mature in autumn; the female cones (**4**) are tightly egg-shaped, with the scales pressed closely against each other, maturing to a length of 10–14cm over two or three years and then disintegrating. A native of the Himalayas, this fast-growing tree is now very commonly planted – usually for ornament, occasionally for timber. It is best distinguished from the other cedars by its drooping main shoot and longer needles.

1

2

3

4

CEDAR OF LEBANON *Cedrus libani*

A massive, squat, almost flat-topped tree (**4**) whose trunk can reach enormous dimensions and is usually complicatedly branched to give a pillar-like effect. The upper branches are normally almost level, the lower ones often drooping and giving a strange effect of dense patches of foliage pierced by large gaps. The bark (**2**) is typically dull grey-brown with long sinuous ridges and the needles (**3**) are shorter, stiffer and usually duller green than a Deodar's. The male cones are greyish and 5cm long; the female cones are similar to the Deodar's but slightly pointed at the tip and pinkish-brown when mature (**5**). Cedar of Lebanon is now extremely rare in its native Near East, but is often planted for dramatic effect rather than ornament.

1

Atlas Cedar *C. atlantica* is readily identifiable in its common blue form *glauca*, (**6**), but mature green trees are difficult to distinguish from Cedar of Lebanon. However, young trees have upward-pointing tips to all shoots, and even older, flatter trees usually retain a trace of a point; in addition the 'short shoots' are longer and the cone (**1**) is smaller. This cedar is a native of the Atlas mountains of North Africa.

2

3

4

5

6

STONE PINE *Pinus pinea*

One of the most characteristic sights of the Mediterranean coast are the groves of Stone Pines (**7**), with their domed crowns casting much valued shade. Stone Pine is characterized by orange-brown bark (**2**) with a few deep vertical cracks, and long (10–20cm) greyish needles in pairs (**6**). The male cones (**3**) are small and orange; the female (**5**) matures into a large, rounded, rather shiny, rich brown cone (**4**), which sheds an economically valuable crop of edible, wingless seeds. Although salt-resistant and much planted on the Mediterranean coast, Stone Pine is frost-sensitive and is therefore scarce further north.

Maritime Pine *P. pinaster* is another Mediterranean coastal pine but with a taller, more open, rather straggly crown. The mature cones (**1**) are much narrower and more conical than in Stone Pine and may stay on the tree for several years before opening. The trunk can be tapped for resin.

1

2

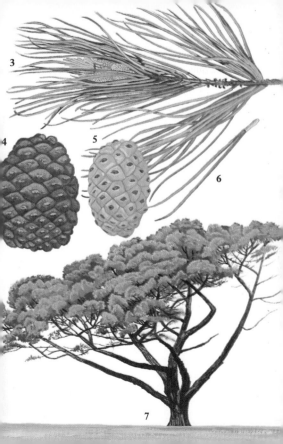

3

4

5

6

7

SCOTS PINE *Pinus sylvestris*

This is the only native British pine and it is found throughout Europe, though only in the mountains in the south. It is a tall tree (**6**), capable of 35–40m, and with very characteristically coloured bark (**2**) on the upper part of the trunk, ranging from rusty brown to orange, and cracked into small, smooth plates. The flat blue-grey needles are 3–7cm long and borne in pairs. The male cones (**3**) are conspicuous as a yellow cluster around the base of the young shoot in May, but soon fall. The female cones (**4**) are initially green, but mature in the third year to give a greyish, oval cone, 4–7cm long (**5**). Scots Pine is an extremely variable tree, growing wild in Scotland in rather open forests with a rich ground flora, and widely naturalized on heaths in England and Wales, when young seedlings (**1**) may be common. It is also often planted both for timber and ornament. The Scottish race has a very conical crown (**7**) and develops the mature shape (**6**), more flat-topped, late; other races remain conical always.

Mountain Pine *P. mugo* is almost a shrub, forming scrub at high altitudes in the Alps. The needles (**8, 9**) are also in pairs. It is often planted.

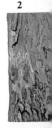

3

4

5

6

7

8

9

AUSTRIAN PINE
Pinus nigra subspecies *nigra*

A magnificent tall pine with a very densely-branched crown (**4**) and very dark bark (**2**). The crown is usually conical, though rather irregular, appearing very dark green or almost black from a distance. The paired leaves are straight and very dark green when young (**1**) but curve inwards and turn almost black with age (**5**); the buds have long pointed tips. The cones (**6**, **7**) are 5–8cm long, suggesting lopsided Scots Pine cones. Austrian Pine is a native of the mountains of central Europe but is now widely planted for ornament and shelter, especially on calcareous soils. Elsewhere, and where planted for forestry, Corsican Pine, subspecies *laricio*, is preferred for its superior timber. Corsican pine is distinguished by its flexible, twisted needles, longer and paler than in Austrian Pine, and its blunter buds. Huge forests of Corsican Pine can be seen, for example, near Thetford and on the Culbin Sands. Male flowers (**3**) are also illustrated.

Shore Pine *P. contorta* is a North American pine which has been planted widely in north and west Britain, at high altitudes and on particularly infertile soils. It has greener foliage (**8**) very short needles (3–6cm), and small, prickly cones (**9**).

74

4

5

6

7

8

9

MONTEREY PINE *Pinus radiata*

This tall, bulky pine with a rounded crown (**5**) hails from a few coastal regions of California and is often planted near western coasts in Britain, where its wind-resistance is its main asset. Its bark (**2**) has deep vertical channels and flakes into intricate patterns. The needles (**1, 4**) are in threes, and are bright green, long (10–15cm) and thin, giving the branches a rather delicate appearance. Monterey Pine has unique cones (**6**) that are retained on the tree and so are always present as a diagnostic feature: they are large, up to 14cm long, and one-sidedly protuberant at the base, owing to the enlargement of the knobs of the cone-scales. Male flowers (**3**) are also illustrated.

Western Yellow Pine *P. ponderosa* is another three-needled pine but with even longer (20cm), dull grey-green needles (**7**). It has a narrower crown, scaly, pinkish or yellowish bark, and mature cones which are slightly smaller (8–12cm) and faintly prickly when mature.

1

2

3

4

5

6

7

AROLLA PINE *Pinus cembra*

Arolla Pine is one of the commoner of the planted pines which have needles in groups of fives. It is usually seen as rather a small tree (rarely over 20m) with a dense, narrow crown (**3**), and it is commonest in northern Europe. In the wild it grows in central Europe at high altitudes, often right up to the tree-line. The bark is gently ridged and scaly. The short (5–8cm) needles (**1**) are dark green on one side and greyish-white on the other, and are borne in dense tufts, on twigs covered with brown fur. The short, squat cones (**2**) are bluey-green at first but ripen to a russet brown.

Weymouth Pine *P. strobus* is another 5-needled pine but its needles (**4**) are up to 12–14cm long. It is a much taller tree, once widely planted as an introduction from eastern North America, and when mature has a rounded crown. It has long but very narrow cones (**4**), often curved at the tip, and hanging from branches.

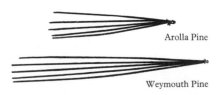

Arolla Pine

Weymouth Pine

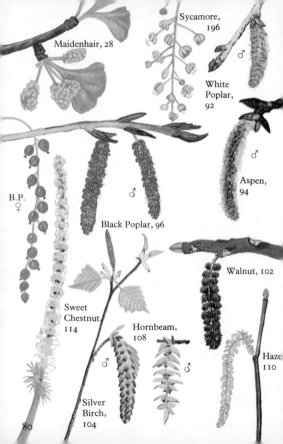

Maidenhair, 28

Sycamore, 196

White Poplar, 92 ♂

B.P. ♀

♂

Black Poplar, 96

Aspen, 94 ♂

Walnut, 102

Sweet Chestnut, 114

Hornbeam, 108 ♂

Hazel 110

Silver Birch, 104

80

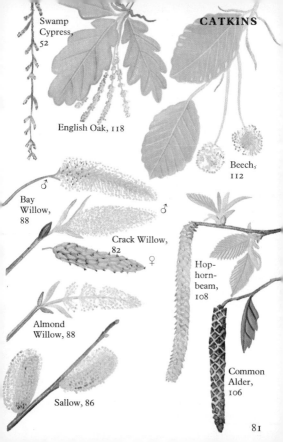

Swamp Cypress, 52

English Oak, 118

CATKINS

Beech, 112

♂ Bay Willow, 88

♂ Crack Willow, 82 ♀

Almond Willow, 88

Hop-hornbeam, 108

Sallow, 86

Common Alder, 106

WHITE WILLOW *Salix alba*

White Willow is a tall, straggly tree reaching 15–20m with long, steeply ascending branches hidden by the striking, dense, silvery-grey foliage (**7**). The trunk has grey-brown, deeply fissured bark (**3**). The leaves (**6**) are long and narrow, tapering to curled tips, and are hairy beneath. The catkins are long and narrow; the males (**4**) have two stamens and are bright yellow in April, while the females (**5**) are green, turning white and fluffy as the downy seeds are shed in June. The buds are long and tightly pressed against the twigs (**1**). White Willow is widespread throughout Europe, though introduced in the north, and found in all parts of Britain. A characteristic riverside tree in lowland areas, it is frequently pollarded on river banks to give an ugly stumpy trunk with tall, narrow ascending shoots. Several varieties are grown, including Golden Osier var. *vitellina* (p. 84) with striking yellow twigs, and var. *coerulea*, the Cricket Bat Willow, which has a tighter crown and bluish leaves; it is grown for making cricket bats.

Crack Willow *S. fragilis* has more spreading branches, brighter green leaves (**8**), and twigs (**2**) that readily break and take root. A confusing range of hybrids are found wherever both parents occur. Male (**9**) and female (**10**) catkins are also illustrated.

WEEPING WILLOW
Salix × chrysocoma

Weeping Willow shares with Monkey Puzzle the distinction of being the easiest tree to identify in Britain; however, there are several types of Weeping Willow whose nomenclature and identification is less simple. The most commonly planted type (**5**) appears to be the hybrid between Golden Osier and the Chinese *S. babylonica* known as *S. × chrysocoma*. It has characteristic long, curved, drooping shoots reaching to the ground and clothed in narrow, softly hairy leaves (**4**); bright yellow twigs (**1**); and usually only male catkins (**3**) which are yellow and curved upwards. The parent, *S. babylonica*, is much rarer and has brown twigs and shorter catkins. Other hybrids occur with White Willow or Crack Willow instead of Golden Osier: these all weep and have some of the characters of the parents.

Golden Osier *S. alba* var. *vitellina* (**6**) is a variety of White Willow (p. 82) and one of two parents of the hybrid Weeping Willow. It is grown for its brilliant yellow twigs (**2**) which are straighter. Its leaves and catkins resemble White Willow.

1

2

SALLOW or PUSSY WILLOW
Salix caprea

Sallow normally forms a large bush but it can produce a respectable trunk and crown up to about 10m (**8**) particularly when growing in woodland. Its branches ascend from a smooth or widely cracked trunk (**3**) and the twigs (**1**) are quite smooth. Sallow has more rounded leaves than any other tree-forming willow, less than twice as long as broad; they are dark green and wrinkled above (**7**), grey and silky beneath (**6**). Male trees are dramatically recognizable in March and April when the large bright yellow catkins (**5**) are in flower; the female trees bear longer (up to 7cm) silky-green catkins (**4**) which explode in May liberating white cottony seeds. Common throughout northern Europe, except in the south west, in damp and dry woods and scrub.

Grey Willow *S. cinerea* is almost always a shrub, but small trees can be recognized by the slightly hairy twigs (**2**), which have small ridges under the bark, and the narrower leaves (**9**), about twice as long as broad. Both subspecies *cinerea* and *atrocinerea* (recognized by the rusty-red hairs under the leaves) occur in Britain, although the latter is more common; usually in wetter places than Sallow. Catkins (**10**) are also illustrated.

ALMOND WILLOW *Salix triandra*

Almond Willow was once widely planted as an osier, when its typical form is a mass of long, ascending shoots rising from a stumpy base, this being the best method of producing the long canes required for basketwork. If left uncut, trees of 10–12m can be seen, somewhat like White Willow in shape. It is best recognized by its flaking, smooth bark (1); its long, narrow, hairless leaves (3) which are about five times as long as broad; and its bright yellow male catkins (4), each flower in which has three stamens, and which are very conspicuous in April. Though well distributed in much of Europe, except in the far north and west, the Almond Willow is often overlooked, and usually found in abandoned osier beds in marshy valleys, and in fens.

Bay Willow *S. pentandra* is usually smaller, even when in tree form. It has fissured bark (2), sticky-looking buds, and more rounded, bay-scented leaves (only about three times as long as broad) dark glossy green above (6) and paler below. It has conspicuous female catkins (7) and the striking male catkins (5) appear in May after the leaves and have five or more stamens in each flower. A characteristic northern and upland plant of lake, streamsides, and moorlands.

OSIER *Salix viminalis*

Osiers are a quite unmistakable feature of lowland Britain, with their immensely long branches (**4**), often arising from pruned stools, and their narrow leaves (**1**), 10–15 times as long as broad, which are white with short, silky hairs underneath, and spread almost horizontally. Catkins are rather inconspicuous, produced in April and May with the leaves, and on very short stalks, so that they tend to be hidden by the long leaves; the male catkins (**3**) are rather stubby and usually only about 3cm long, but the female (**2**) are longer and more cylindrical. Osiers occur naturally by stream-sides and in fens and marshes, and along with many hybrids were formerly extensively planted in special osier beds in wet valleys, now usually degenerated into dense thickets. Common throughout lowland Britain and most of the Continent.

S. eleagnos is another very narrow-leaved willow from central Europe, particularly along river banks in the Alps. It has very narrow, curved catkins. One form, with leaves (**5**) so fine that it has the air of a Tamarisk, is often cultivated.

pruned stools

WHITE POPLAR   *Populus alba*

The poplars are a puzzling group and it is
hard to say which are the true species and
where they are native. White Poplar is certainly introduced in Britain and is probably a
native of south and east Europe. It forms a
medium-sized, little-branched, rather untidy
crown (5), with dark grey-brown, ridged bark
(2). The bark of young trees is whitish with
dark marks. The young twigs (1) are ridged
and white-downy, bearing deeply-lobed
leaves (3) which are dull green on the top and
white underneath. The catkins (4) are very
conspicuous in March and early April, the
males bright reddish-purple with grey hairs
and up to 10cm long, the females greenish
with well-separated flowers. White Poplar is
wind-resistant and suckers freely, so that it is
much planted near the sea, particularly to
stabilize loose sand.

Grey Poplar, *P. canescens* is a larger tree
with less deeply-lobed leaves (6) which are
greyish, not white, underneath. It is probably
a hybrid between White Poplar and Aspen
(p. 94), and is rather more common than the
former.

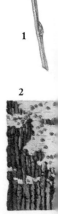

1

2

3

4

5

6

ASPEN *Populus tremula*

The most widespread and the smallest European poplar, rarely exceeding 15m, Aspen (**4**) has smooth silvery-green bark (**2**) which eventually turns brown or greyish and slightly glossy twigs (**1**). It can be instantly recognized by its almost circular, gently scalloped leaves (**3**) which flutter from side to side in the lightest breeze on long leaf stalks. Heart-shaped, untoothed leaves are borne on sucker shoots which grow up around the tree and often form extensive thickets. Before the leaves appear the male trees produce silky, dumpy catkins (**6**), 4–8cm long; female trees have green catkins (**5**) which turn white in May when the woolly seeds are shed (**7**). Aspen is not only widespread geographically, extending from the Arctic to the Mediterranean and right across Asia, but also ecologically. It is most commonly found in wet woods, hedges and screes and on moorland, often in company with Downy Birch (p. 104). In woods its presence is betrayed by its slow-to-rot leaves, which remain yellow in the leaf litter throughout the winter.

1

2

3

4

5

6

7

BLACK POPLAR *Populus nigra*

The black poplars are a confusing group distinguished by their dark, deeply furrowed bark (**2**), finely toothed leaves and almost hairless catkins. The true European Black Poplar is not often seen now but can be instantly recognized by its floppy, rather ungainly crown (**7**), reaching 30–35m, and its massive trunk broken by protruding bosses. It has flat buds (**1**) and bright green, glossy leaves (**5**) with distinctive clear borders and long, stiff stalks. Male trees bear masses of bright red catkins (**4**) in April, before the leaves; the female catkins (**6**) are longer and have widely spaced flowers. Black Poplar may be native in damp woods and by streams in southern England; elsewhere it is found south to the Mediterranean, but the hybrids and varieties below are more often planted.

Lombardy Poplar *P. nigra* var. *italica* has an unmistakable slim outline (**8**). It is always male, has bark with no bosses and is widely planted.

Black Italian Poplar *P.* × *canadensis* var. *serotina* (**9**) is easily confused with Black Poplar but it is usually larger, has no bosses on its trunk (**3**) and a neater crown, with upward-growing branches. A hybrid between *P. nigra* and the American *P. deltoides*, it is widely planted for timber and ornament.

BALM OF GILEAD
Populus × gileadensis

Balm of Gilead is one of the most widely planted of an extremely confusing group of poplars, known as balsam poplars because of the powerful smell emitted by their fat, sticky buds in spring, and detectable from considerable distances. It is a very fast-growing tree, occasionally reaching 30m (**5**) but most often seen as a smaller, neat conical crown, surrounded by suckers (**6**). It has greyish, cracked bark (**2**) and its twigs (**1**) are stout, hairy, and slightly angled. The leaves (**4**) are pale green above and yellowish below, hairy on the veins and somewhat ace-of-spades shaped. It is probably a hybrid between two North American poplars – Eastern Balsam Poplar or Tacamahac, *P. balsamifera*, and Cottonwood, *P. deltoides* – both of which are also sometimes planted here. As a hybrid it has no male catkins, only long green female ones, and reproduces by suckering. It is often planted on industrial wasteland and is sometimes called *P. candicans*, particularly when sold in a variegated form. Tacamahac produces both male and female catkins (**3**).

Western Balsam Poplar *P. trichocarpa* is also from North America, but less often planted. It lacks suckers, but has very angled twigs and leaves (**7**) with straighter bases.

1

2

NUTS

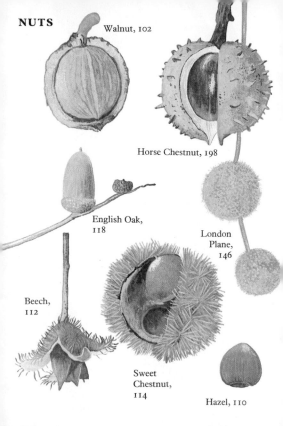

Walnut, 102

Horse Chestnut, 198

English Oak,
118

London
Plane,
146

Beech,
112

Sweet
Chestnut,
114

Hazel, 110

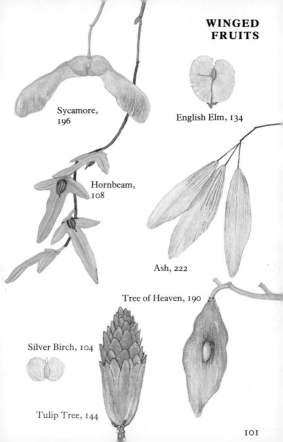

WINGED FRUITS

Sycamore, 196

English Elm, 134

Hornbeam, 108

Ash, 222

Tree of Heaven, 190

Silver Birch, 104

Tulip Tree, 144

101

COMMON WALNUT
Juglans regia

A superb tree, introduced for its delicious fruit from south-east Europe, probably as early as the fifteenth century. Typically Walnuts are grown as single specimen trees, in parks, gardens, or hedgerows, where they produce an expansive crown (**8**), with spreading low branches, but rarely exceed 20m. The trunk can be massive with wide, smooth, grey plates separated by deep fissures (**3**) and the twigs (**2**) are rather thick. The leaves (**4**) are strikingly large and have 7–9 pairs of pointed, leathery, rather dull green leaflets, each up to 15cm long, giving a general impression of a rather overgrown ash leaf, and strongly scented. The male flowers (**6**) are in drooping catkins, but the female flowers (**7**) are in small, inconspicuous groups at the tips of shoots, and ripening to a large green fruit (**1**), 5cm across; inside this lies the famous wrinkled nut (**5**). Widely grown for fruit and timber and occasionally naturalized, Walnut is most recognizable in spring when the leaves open a rich orange.

Black Walnut *J. nigra* is an American walnut, less often encountered, and immediately recognized by its dark, deeply ridged bark, and its lighter green, more delicate leaves (**9**), each with about 15 leaflets.

SILVER BIRCH *Betula pendula*

An elegant, fast-growing tree, rarely surviving more than 100 years, found throughout almost all Europe, and distinguished by its drooping twigs, hanging down from stiffly held main branches (**7**), and by its white, scaly bark (**1**), with conspicuous black patches. Capable of reaching 30m, though rarely seen above 20m, Silver Birch starts out as a neat conical tree, with pinkish brown bark. Leaves (**6**) are oval with a long pointed tip, obviously toothed, but with smaller teeth in between those formed by the main veins. Male catkins (**4**) are 4–5cm long, drooping, yellowish, in small groups; female catkins (**3**) are shorter, green at first in spring and upright, later drooping and turning brown (**5**), shedding masses of tiny winged seeds (**8**) in autumn. Each seed has two papery wings, more than twice as wide as the seed. Silver Birch is a common and characteristic tree of dry, sandy and peaty soils, often seen colonizing heather moor.

1

2

Downy Birch *B. pubescens* has grooved, greyish bark (**2**), not marked as Silver Birch, and spreading branches (**10**). Leaves (**9**) have an abrupt pointed tip and only one row of teeth. The wings of the seeds (**11**) are narrower. As common as Silver Birch, it prefers wetter soils. Hybrids are common.

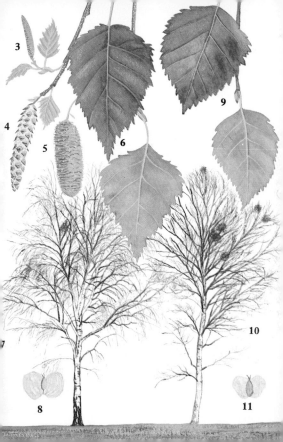

COMMON ALDER *Alnus glutinosa*

One of the commonest waterside trees, Alder rarely reaches 20m, though in cultivation it is capable of 40m. When young, it has an unusually regular conical shape for a non-conifer, but mature trees have rather open, straggly crowns (**7**). Bark (**1**) is grey or brown, with a fine network of shallow fissures. Leaves (**6**) are strikingly rounded, somewhat resembling Hazel (p. 110), but often with an indented tip; bright green and rather shiny, with 4–7 pairs of veins. Male catkins (**4**) are rather like those of the birches, but strikingly contrast purple scales with yellow flowers. Female catkins (**5**) distinguish Alders from all other similar trees, being cone-like (**3**) and remaining on the tree (**2**) long after the tiny winged seeds are shed.

Grey Alder *A. incana* is a European tree, absent only from the north-west, but often planted in land reclamation schemes on colliery spoil heaps. It has smooth, grey bark and pointed, oval leaves (**8**), strongly toothed and greyish beneath. Hybrids with Common Alder occur.

Green Alder *A. viridis* grows mainly in the Alps and in south-east Europe. It has leaves (**9**) intermediate in shape, and catkins in small groups, appearing with the leaves.

1

HORNBEAM *Carpinus betulus*

An attractive tree reaching 30m with steeply ascending branches, often producing a crown widest near the top, and smooth, greyish bark (**1**), sometimes fissured and always buttressed. Young trees are more conical, but short specimens are more likely to have been pollarded (**7**). Leaves (**6**) are rather like those of beech, but with very prominent parallel veins and strongly toothed margins. Male flowers are borne in attractive, short, greenish, rather feathery catkins (**4**). The female catkins (**3**) are very characteristic, short and green, but elongating in fruit, to give instantly recognizable clusters, with each fruit on a 3-lobed wing (**5**). Found in much of Europe, but not in the north and west. Locally common in south-east England, where it forms pure woods, and widely planted elsewhere. Often found as an understorey tree in oakwood.

Hop-hornbeam *Ostrya carpinifolia* is a southern European tree, occasionally planted. It is recognized by its hop-like clusters of very pale yellowish-green fruits (**8**) and finely cracked bark (**2**).

HAZEL   *Corylus avellana*

Hazel is not strictly a tree if we adhere to the requirement for a single trunk, for it almost invariably produces a dense mass of long arching branches (**6**). If left uncut, however, it is capable of producing a trunk and of reaching 8–10m. It is easily recognized at all times of year: in winter by its growth form, its almost yellowish-brown twigs (**1**), and its conspicuous green, rounded buds and immature catkins. In spring it is the familiar yellow male catkins (**2**), 4–7cm long, and maturing at any time from Christmas onwards that are characteristic, while in summer its round, pointed-tipped leaves (**3**), with softly prickly hairs are distinctive. In autumn the well-known clusters of 1–4 nuts (**4**), initially green, but turning brown (**5**) when ripe, and fringed by conspicuous frilly bracts are a familiar sight. Hazel is a very widely distributed shrub in Europe, found all over the British Isles and absent only from the mountains of Scandinavia. In Britain it forms a characteristic shrub layer in oak woods, especially where coppiced to produce the long new twigs for hurdles, wattles, basketry, and the like, but is quite capable of reaching the canopy where the trees are poorly grown. In the extreme west of Britain, especially on sea-cliffs, Hazel forms pure stands, usually shrubby and wind-cut.

1

2

3

4

5

6

BEECH *Fagus sylvatica*

An impressive tree, reaching 30–40m with an enormous, spreading crown (**10**). Its trunk is smooth and grey (**2**), (though mostly green with algae), often branching almost horizontally. The leaves are pointed oval, with veins protruding at the edges. Young leaves are silky underneath, delicate yellow-green (**3**), quickly turning shiny dark green (**5**) and finally rich brown by late autumn (**9**); young trees and hedges retain dead leaves in autumn. Twigs are brown, slightly flexuous, bearing characteristic narrow, pointed buds (**7**). Male flowers are borne in small, rounded catkins, hanging on long stalks (**6**), the females in short-stalked, erect clusters (**4**). The nut is almost pyramidal, glossy brown, and protected by a tough coat (the mast, **8**) which splits into 4 sections and then germinates (**1**) in large numbers the following spring. Native from Spain to south Norway and southern England and often planted further north. Dominant on chalk and some well-drained sands in north-west Europe, but in central Europe more of a mountain tree, forming forests with oak or spruce. Its wood is used for furniture and many ornamental varieties are planted, e.g. Copper Beech.

SWEET CHESTNUT *Castanea sativa*

A handsome and striking tree, frequently growing to about 30m, Sweet Chestnut was almost certainly introduced by the Romans who relied heavily on its nuts and even made flour from them. Although a vigorous tree in Britain, especially on light sandy soils, it has naturalized in surprisingly few places. It forms an even, well-structured crown (**6**) with rather few, but massive spreading branches. The bark (**2**) is quite characteristic with deep, spiral, parallel ridges which usually twist sharply near the ground – and the twigs (**1**) bear large squat buds. Its narrow, dark green, sharply-toothed, glossy leaves (**3**) are among the longest of any tree to be found in Britain (up to 25cm). It produces catkins later than most other trees, on stiff, upright stalks bearing widely spaced male flowers (**5**) and a few small spiky female flowers at the base (**4**). As the female flowers mature into the characteristic green, spiky chestnut fruit (**7**), the male flowers wither but the brown stalk of the catkin projects from the cluster. Each fruit usually has two tough-skinned but richly flavoured nuts (**8**) which unfortunately only mature in favourable years in Britain.

3

4

5

6

7

8

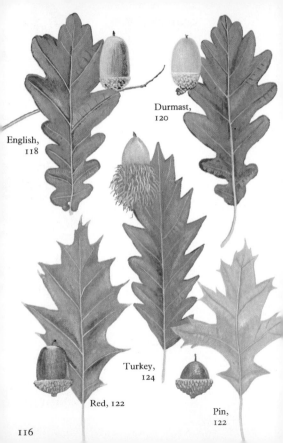

English,
118

Durmast,
120

Turkey,
124

Red, 122

Pin,
122

116

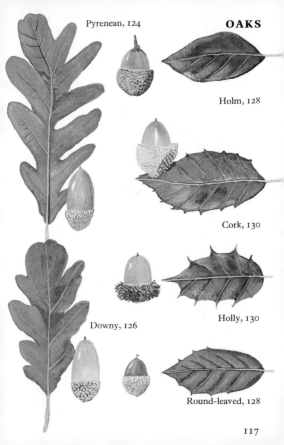

Pyrenean, 124

OAKS

Holm, 128

Cork, 130

Downy, 126

Holly, 130

Round-leaved, 128

ENGLISH OAK *Quercus robur*

Common throughout Europe, except the far north, and the most important forest tree of north-west Europe, English Oak is extremely variable in size and shape, sometimes producing tall, rather ragged crowns, in extreme cases up to 45m high, but more usually a massive, twisted dome (**8**) often less than 20m high when mature. This is because the leading shoot dies (or is eaten); the side shoots then grow off in a different direction, giving branches a succession of dog-legs. The grey bark (**2**) is finely cracked and ridged. The twigs (**3**) bear rounded but pointed buds. English Oak has very short-stalked, but deeply lobed leaves (**6**), with two small backward-pointing lobes at the base. The male catkins (**4**) are conspicuous in short clusters in early May as the leaves unfold; the female catkins (**5**) are similar, but shorter and bearing minute flowers. Fruits are the familiar acorns (**7**), in small clusters on long stalks; jays and squirrels bury them in hoards, so that groups of seedlings (**1**) are sometimes seen. Oak forms extensive woods on heavy land, being replaced by Alder in wet valleys and on dry soils by Beech in the south and Ash, Birch or Pine in the north. In the English Midlands it reigns supreme.

DURMAST or SESSILE OAK

Quercus petraea

Durmast Oak is a very similar tree to English Oak, but rarely forms the massive, low crowns of the latter; it is less prone to zigzag growth so is, typically, a taller, straighter, more elegant tree (5). It is best told from English Oak by its grey-purple twigs (2), its long-stalked leaves (7), lacking the small, backward-pointed lobes, and tapering smoothly onto the stalk, and its unstalked acorns (6) – in other words, the stalk is on the leaves in Durmast Oak and on the acorns in English Oak. The bark (1), too, tends to have longer, straighter fissures and to be less cracked; the male catkins (4) are longer and the female flowers (3) are inconspicuous in the leaf axils. Durmast Oak largely replaces English Oak as the main forest tree on the thinner, acid soils of northern and western Britain, and its woods tend for this reason to be much poorer in associated plants and insects. Indeed, while English Oak is sometimes stripped of leaves by the caterpillars of various moths, particularly the Winter Moth, Mottled Umber, and Green Tortrix, the same fate rarely befalls Durmast Oak.

1

RED OAK *Quercus rubra*

Red Oak is a widely planted North American tree, valuable both economically for its timber and aesthetically for its superb, brilliant orange-red autumn colouring (**7**). Although it is capable of reaching 30–35m, it usually only reaches 20–25m in Britain, with a straight, smooth, silvery trunk (**2**) and massive spreading branches (**8**). The leaves (**5**) are more deeply lobed than in most other oaks, and have fine points at the tips of the lobes. The male flowers (**4**) are borne in conspicuous, slender, yellowish catkins, but the female flowers (**3**) are well-hidden at the base of the leaves and mature over two years to produce a rather rounded acorn (**6**) which sits in a characteristically wide, shallow cup. A winter twig (**1**) is also illustrated.

Pin Oak *Q. palustris* is a similar North American tree, less frequently encountered than the Red Oak, and distinguished from it by its even more deeply lobed leaves (**9**), which have an almost feathery appearance and turn bright scarlet in autumn. It also has somewhat drooping twigs, conspicuous tufts of hairs on the leaves where the veins branch, and smaller (10–15mm) acorn cups. Pin Oak is mainly planted for timber in central Europe and for ornament in Britain.

1

2

4

5

6

7

8

9

TURKEY OAK *Quercus cerris*

An elegant, long-lived tree that produces a tall, domed crown (5), usually borne on a long, straight, unbranched trunk clad in coarsely-fissured grey bark (2), showing orange in the cracks. Turkey Oak can be distinguished from other oaks by the long narrow filaments that surround its leaf buds and which persist to form stipules at the base of the leaves (4). The leaves are dark, dull green, usually hairy underneath, and with deep, regular, near-triangular lobes. Male flowers are produced in dense clusters of dull yellow catkins (3). The oblong acorns in their characteristic bristly, unstalked cups take two years to ripen (as in Red Oak) and so are mature on the old twigs, not on the new growth. Introduced from south-east Europe it is frequently planted and is fully naturalized in southern England, mainly on dry, sandy soils. A winter twig (1) is also illustrated.

Pyrenean Oak *Q. pyrenaica* is a suckering tree with narrower leaf lobes (6), and white down on the leaf undersides. It is late into leaf and produces masses of golden-yellow male catkins and scaly, short-stalked acorns (7). Rarely planted, Pyrenean Oak is a native of southern Europe and naturalized in Belgium.

3

4

5

6

7

DOWNY OAK *Quercus pubescens*

A widespread native tree in central Europe, Downy Oak can reach 20–25m (**5**), but usually only does so in collections or gardens. It is most often encountered as a tall shrub (**6**), with characteristic long grey hairs on its twigs (**1**) and grey, ridged bark (**2**). In many respects it resembles a rather depauperate Durmast Oak (p. 120), but the leaves (**4**) have only shallow lobes, and are covered with dense short hairs underneath, at least in the early part of the season. The male flowers (**3**) are in catkins like those of other oaks. Acorns (**7**) are egg-shaped and borne in small, slightly hairy cups on very short stalks. It is a characteristic small tree or shrub forming low woods on dry, south-facing limestone hillsides primarily in south-east Europe, but scattered north to France, Belgium and Germany, where it is usually accompanied by hybrids with Durmast Oak and sometimes with English Oak as well, making identification difficult. It is occasionally planted in parks.

1

2

HOLM OAK *Quercus ilex*

This is the most frequently encountered evergreen oak in Northern Europe, forming a widely-spreading dome up to 25m high (**5**). Its bark (**1**) is dark grey-brown, almost black from afar, and finely cracked. The leaves (**4**) are evergreen, maturing from shining bright green, through dull green to a very dark colour before being eventually shed; long and narrow, with whitish short hairs underneath and no lobes, except on sucker shoots (**6**). Male flowers (**2**) are borne in long yellow catkins, conspicuous against the dark foliage. The acorns (**3**) are egg-shaped and sit well-exposed in the grey-hairy cup, ripening between May and September. Holm Oak is a common Mediterranean tree, native as far north as Brittany, and widely planted elsewhere, becoming naturalized in southern England.

Round-leaved Oak *Q. rotundifolia* is a smaller tree with broader, rather greyish leaves (**7**), found in south-west Europe.

1

CORK OAK *Quercus suber*

One of the most important economic plants of the Mediterranean, along with the olive and the vine, Cork Oak is easily recognized there by its bright brown trunk where the bark has been removed to give cork. Before stripping, which is done about every twenty years, the trees have thick, deeply fissured grey bark (**1**). Cork Oak is an untidy looking evergreen (**5**) sometimes growing 20m high, though more commonly half that, with small, dark, oval, rather prickly-edged leaves (**2**) with a characteristically zig-zag midrib. The male catkins (**3**) are conspicuous in early spring and the egg-shaped acorns (**4**) sit in fringed cups and ripen the same year. It is mainly grown in Portugal and southern Spain but is planted as far north as southern England.

Spanish Oak *Q.* × *hispanica* is the hybrid with Turkey Oak (p. 124) and is more often seen in England. It is only half evergreen, the leaves falling in spring.

Holly Oak *Q. coccifera* has short-stalked, hairless, prickly leaves (**6**) and is a common scrubby tree in the Mediterranean region.

1

WYCH ELM *Ulmus glabra*

The most easily recognized elm, Wych Elm
(**6**) is distinguished by its large, short-stalked
leaves, and the absence of sucker shoots. The
trunk often forks near the ground and the
bark (**3**) is smooth at first but later develops
thick, straight ribs and turns grey. The leaves
(**5**) vary greatly in shape but are large and very
rough to the touch. As in all elms, the base of
the leaf extends further down the stalk on one
side than the other, but in Wych Elm the long
side crosses over the short stalk and hides it.
The red flowers (**4**) appear in late February
and the winged fruits (**1**), with the seed set
centrally, are visible before the leaves are expanded. Wych Elm is a common woodland
tree, particularly in the north and west, and
has shown considerable resistance to Dutch
Elm disease. Wych derives from an old word
for supple, referring to the twigs (**2**).

Dutch Elm *U.* × *hollandica* is thought to
be a hybrid with *U. minor*. Once common, but
heavily reduced by Dutch Elm disease, it has
cracked bark, many suckers and spreading
branches. Huntingdon Elm var. *vegeta* has
straighter branches but both have longer-
stalked, smoother leaves (**7**) than Wych Elm,
and seeds not in the middle of the fruit.

4

5

6

7

ENGLISH ELM   *Ulmus procera*

English Elm is (or was before the advent of Dutch Elm disease) the classic hedgerow tree of the English lowlands, suckering vigorously to produce long lines of characteristic compact crowns (**6**). It is best distinguished by its small, rounded, rough-surfaced, dark green leaves (**5**), which are longer on one side at the base, but rounded where they join the stalk. It has dark, finely ridged bark (**3**) and slim, hairy twigs (**2**). Red flowers (**4**) are produced in February or March, ripening by May, after the leaves have expanded, to give fruits (**1**) with the seed nearer the top of the round wing. A variable tree with distinct local types maintained by vegetative propagation (suckering). Probably native, but its distribution and origin are imperfectly understood.

Small-leaved Elm *U. minor* typically has narrower leaves (**7**), with the unequal base joining the stalk at right-angles, and oval fruit-wings. It is an exceptionally variable tree, reproducing by suckers to give distinctive local types such as Cornish, Wheatley, and Plot Elms (see pp. 136–7). Common in Europe, and probably introduced in Britain, it is now much reduced by disease.

Fluttering Elm *U. laevis* is a widespread tree of continental Europe with very long-stalked flowers (**8**).

5

6

7

8

ELMS: summer outlines

English, 134

Plot, 134

Small-leaved, 134

Wheatley, 134

Cornish, 134

Huntingdon, 132

Dutch, 132

Wych, 132

SOUTHERN NETTLE TREE
Celtis australis

An elegant tree or shrub, whose rather regular crown (**6**) is usually borne on a long, straight trunk, Southern Nettle Tree has slender, curving branches and twigs (**1**). It has smooth, grey bark (**2**) and distinctive toothed narrow oval leaves (**4**), drawn out into a long curved point and softly hairy on the underside. The flowers (**3**) which appear in March–May, have tiny reddish-brown petals and large, conspicuous styles, but in addition to the normal hermaphrodite flowers with both stamens and styles, each tree bears male flowers as well. It has small fleshy berries (**5**), about 1 cm across, on long flexuous stalks; the young fruits are off-white, ripening through dull red to a dull brownish violet. Widespread in southern Europe, south of the Alps, and west to France, in dry, rocky fields and by streams, often in scrub with plants such as Downy Oak (p. 126) and Flowering Ash (p. 222). Occasionally planted further north.

1

2

hermaphrodite flower

3

4

5

6

BLACK MULBERRY *Morus nigra*

A short, unimpressive tree (5) rarely reaching 10m, Black Mulberry nevertheless often has a disproportionately massive trunk, with bright reddish-brown, extensively fissured bark (2), and often massive protruding bosses. Mulberries have large, oval leaves (3) up to 20cm long, with toothed margins sometimes deepening into lobes, and fat, slightly hairy twigs (1). Males and female flowers are separate but on the same tree and have all their parts in fours; they open in May. The fruits (4) are unmistakable, resembling firm, juicy raspberries, ripening from green to vermilion to a deep dark purple in late summer and then sweet and edible. Black Mulberry is a native of central Asia, widely planted for its fruits as far north as southern England.

White Mulberry *M. alba* is a slightly taller and more elegant tree with slender branches and hairless leaves (6) and twigs. Its fruits (7) vary from whitish to purple and are stalked. A Chinese species once cultivated as the food-plant for silkworms in southern Europe, but now less often seen than Black Mulberry.

1

2

3

4

5

6

7

FIG *Ficus carica*

The fig is an unmistakable tree with its large (20cm long), prominently but shallowly lobed, slightly greyish-green leaves (**3**) and its rather lumpy appearance (**6**). It has smooth, shiny, pale grey bark, on a short trunk which usually branches quite close to the ground. In winter the stubby, ridged twigs (**2, 5**) with their large green terminal bud are distinctive, as is the fleshy, green fig itself (**4**) in which the separate male and female flowers are concealed. In the Mediterranean pollination is achieved by a minute gall-wasp which lays its eggs in some of the female flowers which have short styles and, in so doing, pollinates other flowers with longer styles; these mature and the fig begins to ripen, turning from green to purple-brown in the second year and swelling to 5–8cm (**1**). The Fig is widely cultivated and naturalized in southern Europe, and planted in sheltered spots as far north as northern England.

variation in lobing

TULIP TREE *Liriodendron tulipifera*

This fine tree is important in forests in the eastern United States, and has quite unmistakable lobed leaves (**4**) ending in a V-shaped notch, rather than a point. It forms a tall narrow crown (**5**) with branches curving downwards and then sharply up, supported by a massive trunk, coated with grey, cracked bark (**2**). The twigs (**1**) bear long reddish, often curved buds. The large flowers (**3**), about 6cm across, are produced in June, and have broad, curving, cup-like, green and orange petals, surrounding the rings of thick, fleshy, yellowish stamens. The fat green 'cone' in the centre ripens to produce a cluster of winged, brown fruits, which remain on the tree for some months. Planted and common in parks to quite far north in Scotland.

Magnolias are closely related trees, usually with simple pointed oval leaves (**7**). Some also have greenish flowers, but those most often planted have huge white or pink flowers, 10–15cm across (**6**). Commonest is *Magnolia × soulangeana*, but *M. stellata* with narrow petals, and the evergreen *M. grandiflora*, usually trained against a wall, are also not infrequently seen.

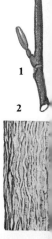

1

2

3

4

5

6

7

LONDON PLANE
Platanus × *hispanica*

London Plane is one of the few trees that can be identified with ease from its bark (**2**) alone, which is greyish-brown but flakes off to leave large yellowish patches. It forms a tall stately tree (**6**) but is often also seen pollarded and cut back. Its large rufous buds (**1**) have a small peg (the old leaf-scar) at their bases. The pure green leaves (**4**) have five well-marked pointed lobes each itself lined with large teeth; they appear late, usually towards the end of May. The deep purplish-red female flowers (**3**) are borne in small round balls on long stalks at the same time as the leaves and mature to give the familiar rough football-like plane fruits (**5**). The seeds are rarely viable, however, for London Plane is a hybrid between two trees, the Oriental Plane *P. orientalis* of Asia and south-east Europe, and the American Plane *P. occidentalis*. Where and when the hybrid appeared is a matter of controversy but it has proved without equal in withstanding the vicissitudes of city life – air pollution, poor soils etc – and has become one of the most familiar of urban trees.

COMMON PEAR *Pyrus communis*

A straggling tree (**6**), usually 10–15m high. In winter the stubby 'short shoots' give the whole tree a bristly appearance. It has dark, scaly, fissured bark (**2**) and rather yellowish twigs (**1**). The rounded oval leaves (**4**) are glossy, woolly beneath when young, but finally hairless, and borne on long stalks. It flowers earlier than the superficially similar Crab Apple (p. 152), nearly always in April, sometimes by late March, when the leaves are just emerging; flowers (**3**) are large, up to 4cm across, in loose, flat-topped heads, and have conspicuous purple anthers. The Common Pear is the parent of all cultivated pears but in the wild it has small, hard, often rounded fruits (**5**), less than 4cm long which can litter the ground below; cultivated varieties can have fruits up to 15cm long, ripening soft. Its origin and native range are unknown; now a widely distributed but never common hedgerow tree, from northern England southwards.
Wild Pear *P. cordata* is a thorny shrub found in western France and near Plymouth. It has a pointed flowerhead, smaller flowers, and a round, finally red fruit, less than 2cm (**7**).
Willow-leaved Pear *P. salicifolia* is often planted. Normally weeping, it has narrow, greyish leaves (**8**).

1

2

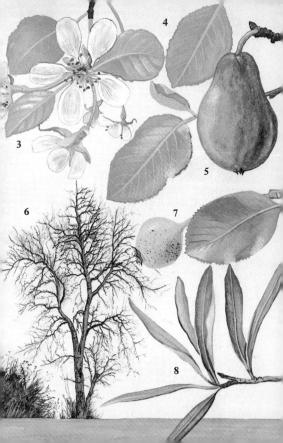

3   4   5   6   7   8

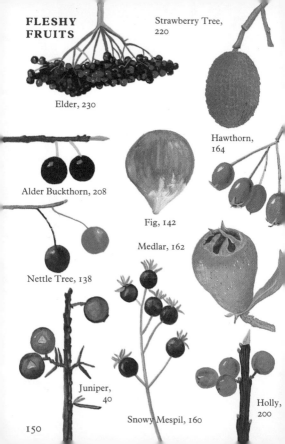

FLESHY FRUITS

Strawberry Tree, 220

Elder, 230

Hawthorn, 164

Alder Buckthorn, 208

Fig, 142

Medlar, 162

Nettle Tree, 138

Juniper, 40

Snowy Mespil, 160

Holly, 200

150

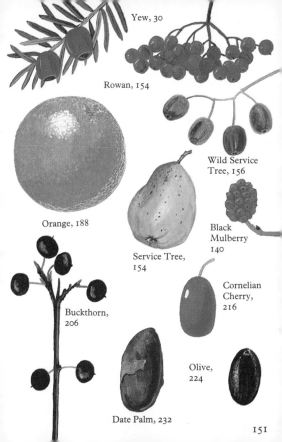

Yew, 30

Rowan, 154

Wild Service Tree, 156

Orange, 188

Service Tree, 154

Black Mulberry 140

Buckthorn, 206

Cornelian Cherry, 216

Olive, 224

Date Palm, 232

CRAB APPLE   *Malus sylvestris*

Crab Apple is an often shrubby tree (**6**) common in hedges and woodland edges, but also occurring as a true woodland tree, mainly in oakwoods. Its scaly bark (**2**) is often paler and smoother than that of Common Pear (p. 148) and it rarely exceeds 10m. It has rounded or oval leaves (**4**) which open woolly, but expand hairless, all borne on the stubby short shoots or spurs (**1**). The large flat, white or pink 5-petalled flowers (**3**) can be up to 6cm across, in small flattened clusters, and appear after the leaves in May. The small fruits (**5**), about 2cm across, yellow when ripe, and sour, are borne on hairless stalks. Crab Apple occurs throughout Europe, north to southern Scotland.

Cultivated Apple *M. domestica* occurs in so many varieties that a single description is impossible, but all have leaves (**7**) that remain woolly on the underside, and hairy stalks to the large, sweeter fruits (**8**) which may be red, green or yellow.

ROWAN *Sorbus aucuparia*

Rowan is an elegant, slender tree (**6**), reaching 15m or rarely more, and with steeply ascending branches. It has smooth, shining, grey-brown bark (**2**) until quite old, and distinctive pinnate leaves (**4**), typically with 6–7 pairs of leaflets. Young twigs (**1**) are slightly hairy, and the buds extremely so when bursting. The attractive creamy flowers (**3**) are produced in May, each less than 1cm across, but in dense flat-topped heads, 10–15cm across, usually stiffly erect and conspicuous. Fruits (**5**) almost spherical, 6–9mm, bright scarlet in August. An important native tree of the whole European continent, but particularly common in the north and in mountain regions, and there reaching higher than other deciduous trees. Usually on infertile soils, often in areas of high rainfall, and common in upland moors and rocky slopes. Widely planted for its supposedly beneficial effect in driving away witches.

True Service Tree *S. domestica* is a more massive tree with spreading branches, best distinguished by rough, scaly bark, larger flowers and larger, yellow-brown pear-shaped fruits (**7**). Widespread in southern Europe and occasionally planted further north.

1

2

3

4

5

6

7

WILD SERVICE TREE
Sorbus torminalis

This unusual looking tree is often a puzzle
when first seen, with its combination of
deeply lobed leaves, somewhat resembling
those of Plane (p. 146), white flowers, and
small brown fruit. It has a neat crown and can
reach 25m; the bark (2) is flaking and lightly
fissured. Its buds (1) are rounded and a striking clear green, and the glossy green leaves (4)
are up to 10cm long, with 2–5 pairs of long-
pointed toothed lobes, the whole leaf roughly
triangular in shape. The white flowers (3) are
larger than those of Rowan (p. 154) and in
more open clusters, and appear in May and
June. Fruit (5) ripens in September, bright
brown, oblong and rough-marked. A very
widely distributed European tree, north to
central England, but typically found as isolated individuals, often in clearings in woods
on damp, rather infertile soils. In Britain,
usually associated with English Oak (p. 118)
and on the continent often with Downy Oak
(p. 126).

1

2

WHITEBEAM   *Sorbus aria*

In the open Whitebeam produces a regular crown (**8**) up to 20m high, but in woods it forms a mass of steeply rising branches. The bark (**4**) is smooth grey-brown until quite old and buds (**3**) are long. The distinctive leaves (**7**) are usually oval, dull green above with thick white hairs beneath so that in wind the whole tree seems pale grey. The leaf margins are toothed, not lobed. Leaf characters distinguish a large number of closely-related species, mostly very rare. The small white flowers (**5**), about 15mm across, appear in loose, domed clusters in May and June, and the scarlet, spherical or oblong fruits (**6**) by September. Typical of woods and scrub on chalk and limestone in western Europe, north to central England; related species occur in Scotland and Scandinavia.

Swedish Whitebeam *S. intermedia* is a native of Scandinavia but is widely planted and often naturalized. It has deeply lobed leaves (**9**), grey (not white) beneath and larger fruits (**1**). Again many rare allied species occur.

Broad-leaved Whitebeam *S. × latifolia* is a widely planted hybrid of Whitebeam and Wild Service Tree (p. 156), with shallow leaf-lobes (**10**) and orange-brown fruits (**2**). It resembles some of the rare native whitebeams.

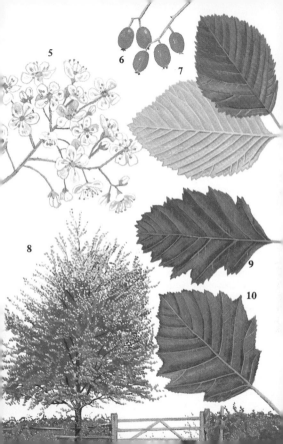

SNOWY MESPIL *Amelanchier laevis*

A startlingly beautiful tree when in flower,
Snowy Mespil is perhaps most often seen as a
straggling shrub (**5**) but occasionally reaches
10–12m when it has a smooth, dark trunk (**2**).
It usually forms a dense tangle of long shoots,
branching from close to the ground, and lacking thorns but with narrow, pointed buds (**1**).
The leaves (**4**) are 5–6cm long, oval, but
pointed, and edged with fine, even teeth.
When first expanding in April they are strongly
purplish and form a striking background to
the mass of white flowers. Flowers (**3**) have
long narrow petals up to 2cm, and are borne
on long spikes, rising away from the branches.
The small spherical fruits (**6**), 5–6cm in
diameter, ripen through red to a deep, dark
purple. A North American plant of doubtful
origin, widely grown in parks and gardens,
and sometimes naturalized, for example in
Surrey. The shrubby *A. ovalis* grows in rocky
places in central Europe; it has more coarsely
toothed leaves. *A. grandiflora*, another North
American species, often grown in gardens and
occasionally naturalized, has larger, shorter-
stalked fruits.

1

2

MEDLAR *Mespilus germanica*

A curious looking, usually spiky shrub which, when cultivated, can be a small tree 5–6m high, with greyish, flaking bark (**1**) revealing more brightly-coloured patches. The narrow leaves (**3**), 10–15cm long, are a dull, almost olive-green above, and wrinkled and leathery; hairy below, and very short-stalked. The large white flowers (**2**), 4–6cm across, appear singly in May, and the narrow, pointed sepals protrude between the petals. The hard, greenish, brown fruits (**4**) are spherical at the base but flat-topped and crowned by the sepals. Native in south-eastern Europe but cultivated since medieval times in western Europe and occasionally naturalized, most often in hedges.

1

winter silhouette

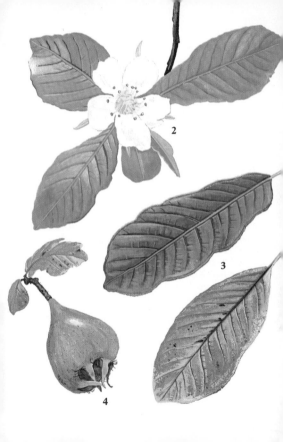

2

3

4

HAWTHORN *Crataegus monogyna*

One of the most familiar sights of lowland Europe, Hawthorn is typically seen as a dense thorny shrub, but will readily form a small tree (**9**) up to 12m high, with bright brown, flaking bark (**5**). Leaves (**7**) variable but lobed at least half-way to the midrib, normally with 3–4 pairs of lobes. The flowers (**6**) appear in dense clusters in late May and early June, each 10–15mm across, white, but turning pink as they mature; occasional pink or double-flowered forms occur and are much planted. Each flower has only one style (**1**) and one ovary (**3**) (hence *monogyna*). Fruits (**8**) are the familiar haws, deep red, sometimes purplish, ripe in September, but persisting on the trees if not stripped by birds. Common on all soils except the most acid, and the commonest hedge plant except in towns, where it has been supplanted by the monotony of Privet and Leyland Cypress.

Midland Hawthorn *C. laevigata* is more of a woodland plant (**13**) and has leaves (**11**) lobed less than half-way to the midrib and flowers (**10**) with two styles (**2**) and ovaries (**4**). In Britain it is found mainly in the southeast growing with *C. monogyna* and hybridizing freely, but flowering a week or so earlier. Fruits (**12**) are also illustrated.

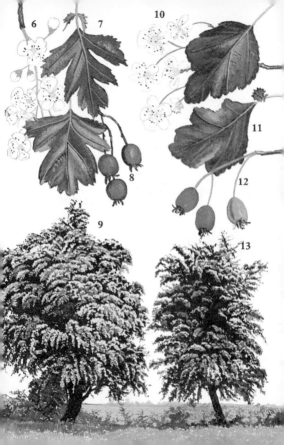

NB: not to scale

Almond, 168

Peach, 170

Apricot, 170

Sloe, 172

Cherry-plum, 174

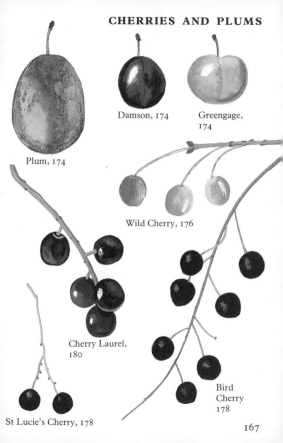

CHERRIES AND PLUMS

Plum, 174

Damson, 174

Greengage, 174

Wild Cherry, 176

Cherry Laurel, 180

St Lucie's Cherry, 178

Bird Cherry 178

ALMOND *Prunus dulcis*

One of the many fruit trees whose cultivation is so ancient that the native range is unknown, Almond is unusual amongst its relatives in being grown for its nut rather than the fleshy fruit. Most often seen as a small tree (**6**), 5–10m high, it has very dark bark (**3**), and wild trees, in southern Europe, have spiny twigs. The leaves (**5**) are narrow, 7–12cm long, and spear-shaped, with a finely toothed margin; typically folded along the midrib. One of the earliest suburban trees to flower, in March, its strong pink flowers (**4**) are 3–5cm across and conspicuous on the leafless branches. The well-known nut (**1**) is concealed in a flattened green fruit (**7**) and may persist so on the tree during winter. Probably native to western Asia, but commonly planted, both for ornament in northern Europe, and also for the nut crop in the south. A winter twig (**2**) is also illustrated.

1

2

3

spiny twig

APRICOT *Prunus armeniaca*

This small tree is seen as an orchard crop in southern Europe but further north most often trained against a south facing wall. It has long-stalked oval leaves (**4**) with very finely toothed margins and delicate pink flowers (**3**) which appear on the bare twigs in March and April, often clustering at the tips of the twigs. The striking 'apricot' coloured fruit (**5**) is fleshy and rounded, with a well-marked notch, and a soft heavy coat; it ripens early – in June in the Mediterranean. Apricot is probably a native of Asia. A winter twig (**1**) is also illustrated.

Peach *P. persica* is slightly more hardy and can be found in cultivation further north and in sheltered corners north to Scotland. It has long narrow leaves (**6**), resembling Almond, p. 168, but broadest above the middle, and thin flexible twigs (**2**). The flowers (**7**) are a deeper pink than Apricot and appear slightly later as the leaves unfold; it has a very familiar and distinctive fruit (**8**), larger than an Apricot and pinker. Probably a native of China. A winter twig (**2**) is also illustrated.

Other *Prunus* species are planted for their fruits, such as Nectarine, whose fruit resembles a small, glossy peach, or for ornament, including a very wide range of Japanese cherries.

1

2

BLACKTHORN   *Prunus spinosa*

Blackthorn rarely forms a tree and is typically
seen as an occasional plant in a hawthorn
hedge, or as a densely tangled thicket (**5**); up
to 4m tall, it is by far the commonest and
most widespread European *Prunus*. Quickly
recognized by its very dark thorny shoots
(**1**) (hence 'Blackthorn'), which contrast
strongly with the dense clusters of small
white flowers which appear before the leaves,
usually in late March or early April. The
leaves (**3**) are small (2–4cm), narrow, oval
and finely toothed. Individual flowers (**2**)
are 12–15mm across, clustered on the short
shoots, and with conspicuous red anthers.
The fruits (**4**) are the familiar sloes, firm
rounded blue-black plums, about 1cm across,
with an attractive purplish bloom and very
bitter flesh; they are conspicuous from late
August to October. Blackthorn is a native
plant found throughout Britain in scrub,
hedges and woodland edges, and occasionally
persisting inside woods in shade. It will grow
on almost any soil except for that of wet, acid
peat-bogs.

2

3

4

5

CHERRY-PLUM or MYROBALAN PLUM *Prunus cerasifera*

A shrub or small, rough-barked (**1**) tree usually less than 10m high (**6**), Cherry-plum stands out in March as the first white-flowered blossom tree, flowering several weeks before Blackthorn, and at the same time as the young leaves (**2**). The shiny, sometimes spiny twigs stay green until their third year and bear pointed oval leaves (**4**) up to 7cm long. The flowers (**3**) resemble those of Blackthorn but occur in sparser groups and are larger, about 2cm across. The rather pinkish red, cherry-like fruits (**5**) only mature in a hot summer in Britain. A native of south-eastern Europe but widely planted and usually found near houses, often in a purple-leaved form (var. *atropurpurea*).

Wild Plum *P. domestica* probably derives from a hybrid of Cherry-plum and Blackthorn. It has grey-brown twigs and flowers later, in April and May. One type, Bullace, ssp *instititia*, has downy twigs, small purple-black fruits, is often naturalized, and is probably the parent of the cultivated Damson. The Garden Plum, ssp. *domestica*, has greenish-white flowers and larger fruits of various colours: green (greengage (**8**)), purple (Czar), reddish-orange (Victoria (**7**)), etc.

1

WILD CHERRY or GEAN
Prunus avium

Wild Cherry is much the most impressive tree amongst all its relatives, regularly reaching 20m or more, with purple-grey, shiny, peeling, horizontally-banded bark (2) coating the regular cylindrical trunk, often buttressed at the base. Open-grown trees have neat conical crowns (7). The buds are large, pointed and conspicuously russet against the grey twigs (1) and burst in April unfolding leaves that are initially bronze (6) and soon turn green. Leaves (5) typically hang limply and have two prominent knobs where they join the stalk. The large, long-stalked, cup-shaped flowers (3) open in small clusters in April before or at the same time as the leaves. Double-flowered forms are often planted. The fruit (4) is a familiar cherry, ripening through yellow and bright red to dark purplish-red, but much favoured by birds. Wild Cherry grows throughout Europe. It is characteristic of wood-edges but can grow in full canopy, often in beechwoods.

Sour Cherry *P. cerasus* is a shrubby plant with smaller, darker, short-stalked leaves (8) and rounded petals. Much cultivated – its varieties comprise most of the edible cherries (9) – it is widely but sparsely naturalized.

BIRD CHERRY *Prunus padus*

Bird Cherry forms a small bushy tree (**6**) up to
15m high, and frequently leafy almost to the
ground. It has smooth, dark, aromatic bark
(**2**) with prominent orange flecks and brown
twigs (**1**). Leaves (**4**) are usually smaller than
in Wild Cherry and are dark green and
leathery, with conspicuous reddish petioles.
Bird Cherry is best recognized by having its
flowers (**3**) on long stiff spikes and not in
clusters, from 10–35 on each spike. Individual flowers appear in May and are small,
10–15mm across, with slightly ragged petals,
and mature to give shiny black cherries (**5**),
6–8mm across. This is the commonest cherry
in Scotland and the upland parts of northern
England, and occurs through much of
Europe, south to the Alps. It grows in open,
rocky woods, by streams and in limestone
pavements.

St Lucie's Cherry *P. mahaleb* is shrubbier,
with small, rounded leaves, short spikes of
only 3–10 flowers (**7**) and slightly larger fruits
(**8**). It grows in dry scrub in central Europe,
extending to Belgium.

Black Cherry *P. serotina* is a North American tree, often planted, which has dense
spikes of smaller flowers and purplish-black
fruits.

1

2

3 4 5 6 7 8

CHERRY LAUREL
Prunus laurocerasus

Cherry Laurel is a widely planted and frequently naturalized shrub or small tree (**5**) that is regularly mistaken for a Rhododendron (p. 218). It has dark grey bark (**1**) with small orange cracks and long (up to 20cm) glossy, stiff, rather brittle leaves (**3**), on short green stalks, less than 1cm long. The flowers (**2**) appear in April and May, each 8–10mm across, on erect, 8–12cm long spikes, ripening to give shiny purplish-black oblong cherries (**4**) 10 by 15mm, in September. Though native only in south-east Europe, Cherry Laurel has been widely planted in western Europe and is often found as an understorey shrub, naturalized in woods in western Britain. The leaves produce cyanide when crushed.

Portugal Laurel *P. lusitanica* is the other evergreen cherry that is sometimes planted in western Europe. It is a larger tree than Cherry Laurel, and its dark green leaves have red stalks up to 2.5cm long. Flowers (**6**) and fruit (**7**) are both smaller, usually failing to mature. It is a native in Spain and Portugal but rarely naturalized in Britain.

1

2

3

4

6

5

7

LABURNUM *Laburnum anagyroides*

A small tree (**6**) up to 8–10m high with
smooth brownish-green bark (**2**) and green,
hairy twigs (**1**), Laburnum is one of the most
conspicuous features of the urban scene in
late May and early June. The leaves (**4**) are
compound, each with 3 leaflets, slightly
hairy beneath. The flowers (**3**) are dramatic,
densely borne on long hanging spikes up to
25cm long, and sometimes almost covering
the tree. Individual flowers are the characteristic pea-flower shape, about 2cm long. The
dry, brown pods (**5**) open violently, throwing
out the seeds. The whole tree, but particularly the seeds, is extremely poisonous. Laburnum is native in southern and central
Europe, mainly in open woods and scrub in
hilly areas. Very widely planted in Britain, it
is often found bird-sown far from houses.

Scotch Laburnum *L. alpinum* has smaller
flowers (**8**) in longer spikes, opening a few
weeks later. Leaves (**7**) are larger and they and
the twigs are hairless. Native in the Alps and
surrounding area and planted mainly in Scotland. The hybrid between these, with long
spikes of larger flowers and pods almost without seeds, is widely planted.

Judas Tree *Cercis siliquastrum* is a Mediterranean tree with heart-shaped leaves (**9**) and
pink flowers.

1

2

3

4

5

6

7

8

9

LOCUST TREE *Robinia pseudoacacia*

Locust Tree or False Acacia was one of the
first North American trees to be introduced to
this country where it thrives when planted in
light soils, but only infrequently seeds itself.
In southern Europe it is widely naturalized. It
forms a massive tree (**7**), to 25m, with very
rough, coarsely-ridged, shredding bark (**3**).
The reddish twigs (**2**) bear pairs of spines and
pinnate leaves (**6**) with 3–10 pairs of leaflets.
The white flowers (**5**) appear in June in long
(to 20cm) hanging spikes, ripening to give
flattened pods (**1**) 5–10cm long.

Pagoda or Scholar's Tree *Sophora japonica* is a superficially similar tree with no
spines, narrower leaflets (**8**) and bark with
broad, ridges. The creamy white flowers appear in upright spikes much later in the year.
A Chinese tree, occasionally planted.

Honey-locust *Gleditsia triacanthus* is
another North American tree usually recognized by the clusters of long, branched
spines on its trunk (**4**), but spineless forms are
planted. Male and female flowers are in separate spikes, ripening to give long twisted
pendulous brown pods, which stay on the tree
in the winter. Its leaves (**9**) are yellow-green.

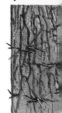

All have simply pinnate leaves in contrast to
Acacias which have bipinnate leaves (**10**).

5 6

7

8

9

10

MIMOSA *Acacia dealbata*

Acacias are widely planted in the Mediterranean but are not hardy and so are seldom seen in Britain outside Devon and Cornwall. The best known is Mimosa, an extremely delicate small tree (**4**) with smooth brown bark and feathery leaves (**1**) which are pinnate with pinnate leaflets. There may be up to 20 pairs of leaflets, each with up to 50 pairs of short leaflets only 3–4mm long, giving an ethereal appearance. The pale yellow flowers (**2**) are in small ball-like heads 5–6mm across, in long clusters, produced very early in the year. The flattened brown pods (**3**) are up to 10cm long.

Blackwood Acacia *A. melanoxylon* is a tree up to 40m tall which has similar leaves when young, but when mature has simple oblong leaves (**5**). The flower-heads are larger and white. Planted in south-west Europe.

Many other *Acacias* are planted in southern Europe and occasionally naturalized.

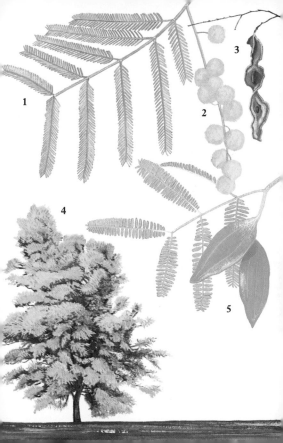

CITRUS

The familiar citrus fruit include half a dozen or so types that are grown in Europe. All are closely related and several may be grafted onto a single stock. In addition to the familiar oranges, lemons, and grapefruit, the large-fruited citron *Citrus medica* and shaddock *C. grandis* are sometimes grown, the latter resembling an almost spineless grapefruit *C. paradisi*. The tangerine *C. deliciosa* is also sometimes found.

Sweet Orange *Citrus sinensis* is the most widely cultivated species, however, being planted in large groves in the Mediterranean region. It is a small evergreen tree (**4**) with weak spines and pointed, leathery, dark leaves (**2**) on winged stalks. The flowers (**1**) appear in short spikes in April and are white and strongly fragrant. The familiar fruits (**3**) are solid at the core.

Seville Orange *C. aurantium* is the best marmalade orange, with acid juice and a hollow in the centre of the thick-rinded fruit (**5**). Leaves have broad wings to the stalk where it joins the leaf.

Lemon *C. limon* (**6**) has some flowers only male and stronger spines. Leaf-stalks hardly winged. Lemon has many more stamens than other *Citrus* species except for the very similar sweet lime *C. limetta*.

TREE OF HEAVEN
Ailanthus altissima

A tall, elegant tree (**4**), frequently reaching 20m and occasionally more, it has a long, unbranched trunk clothed in smooth grey bark. Tree of Heaven is late into leaf, remaining bare until June and then unfolding large, pinnate ash-like leaves (**3**) each with 6–12 pairs of leaflets up to 12cm long, the whole leaf being as long as 60cm. The leaflets are toothed at the base and glossy and wrinkled on the top surface. The twigs (**1**) are fat and orange, and have prominent leaf-scars, somewhat reminiscent of Horse Chestnut (p. 198). It has both separate male and female flowers and normal hermaphrodite ones, and individual trees may be wholly male, wholly female, or somewhere in between. The flowers (**2**) open in July, each 7–8mm across, greenish-white, in long branching spikes on the ends of the shoots. The fruits (**5**) are winged, each with a central seed, again rather similar to Ash (p. 222), but ripening to a bright reddish brown in September. It is a native of China, but it is widely planted, particularly in towns as it seems resistant to aerial pollution, and it is occasionally naturalized.

1

2

3

4

5

NORWAY MAPLE *Acer platanoides*

A widespread but often overlooked tree, Norway Maple suddenly becomes very conspicuous for a few weeks in early April when the striking golden-yellow flowers open, on bare brown twigs. It forms a fine tree up to 30m tall (**5**) with a short unbranched trunk clad in grey, smooth or finely-ridged bark (**2**). The twigs (**1**) and leaves (**4**) are both hairless, the latter a bright pure green with 5 fine-pointed toothed lobes giving a delicate, somewhat spiky appearance. The small flowers (**3**) (8mm across) are borne in upright clusters containing both male and female flowers, open before the leaves expand and before the flowers of the related Sycamore (p. 196). The typical winged maple fruits (samaras) are olive-coloured and occur in pairs (**6**), the wings making an angle of 150°. A native tree of Scandinavia and the European mountains, Norway Maple is often planted, sometimes in dark-leaved or variegated forms, and the typical form readily seeds itself.

1

2

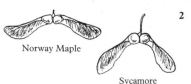

Norway Maple

Sycamore

FIELD MAPLE *Acer campestre*

A small, rather ungainly tree (**6**) usually
10–15m high, though rarely as much as 25m,
Field Maple is also a common hedgerow
shrub. The trunk bears fissured, flaky, grey-
brown bark (**2**), orange-brown when freshly
exposed. The young twigs (**1**) are slightly
hairy and the small (4–8cm) deep green leaves
(**4**) have 5 (occasionally 3) rounded lobes, and
are downy on the underside; in autumn they
turn a deep golden-red. It bears separate male
and female flowers (**3**) on each tree, both in
sparse, upright clusters which appear in May
after the leaves have opened. The fruits (**5**) are
in pairs whose wings spread almost horizontally at an angle of nearly 180°. Field Maple is
a common tree of lowland England, in woods
and old hedges, and extends south to the
Mediterranean, though there rarely and in
hilly areas.

Montpelier Maple *A. monspessulanum* is
usually smaller and has the wings of the pairs
of fruits almost parallel (**8**), and sometimes
reddish. Otherwise it resembles a Field
Maple with darker, somewhat leathery,
three-lobed leaves (**7**). It grows in dry scrub
throughout the Mediterranean and north to
West Germany, and is occasionally planted
elsewhere.

1

2

3

4

5

6

7

8

SYCAMORE *Acer pseudoplatanus*

Sycamore is by far the commonest maple in Britain. It forms a magnificent domed tree (7) up to 35m tall with bark (3) that starts smooth and grey but soon cracks and finally becomes flaking and rough. The twigs (2) are stout and bear fat, green buds. The large (up to 15cm) dark green leaves (6) have 5 pointed toothed lobes, and are almost invariably seen (except in towns) blotched by the fungus *Rhytisma acerinum* and often by crimson galls. The flowers (4) hang in long spike-like clusters, up to 100 in each, appearing in April along with the leaves. The pairs of fruit (5) have wings at about 90°, and after falling germinate in vast numbers the following spring to give the familiar seedlings (1). A native tree of the central and northern European mountains, it is introduced in Britain where it has become an essential part of the British scene and is often the most vigorous tree in upland areas. Ecologically it somewhat resembles Ash (p. 222).

Italian Maple *A. opalus* is a smaller Mediterranean tree, with wings of the fruit (9) making an angle of about 30° or less. It has larger flowers and smaller leaves (8) with shallower lobes.

4

5

6

7

8

9

HORSE CHESTNUT
Aesculus hippocastanum

One of the most familiar trees in areas near houses, Horse Chestnut is not in fact a native of Britain, but was introduced from southeast Europe in the seventeenth century. It forms a billowing, spreading, dome (6) typically up to 25m high but occasionally as much as 35m, on a massive trunk with bark (3) cracking off in long plates. Its rich brown buds (2) are large, up to 3.5cm long, and sticky, bursting to unfold the unmistakable oval leaflets (5), up to 25cm long. Most trees flower in May, though some are early into leaf (in March) and flower (in April), becoming covered with the tall upright candelabras (1) of white, unequally 5-petalled flowers (7), each crimson blotched in the centre. In late September the mature fruits (4) fall, their green spiny shells splitting to reveal 1–3 shiny brown nuts. The name chestnut derives from the resemblance to the true, edible Chestnut (p. 114); Horse Chestnuts are inedible but very hard, and possessed of qualities endearing them to children. Very commonly planted and often naturalized.

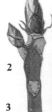

Pink Horse Chestnut *A.* × *carnea* is smaller and often poorly grown, with pink flowers (8). It is often planted.

HOLLY *Ilex aquifolium*

Holly is not a tree that can be readily confused with any other. The tough, shiny, dark green leaves (**2**) have undulating margins, normally lobed and with the lobes ending in stiff, sharp spines. Upper leaves and, rarely, those of all or most of the tree may be spineless and almost smooth-edged (**4**), possibly leading to confusion with evergreen oaks, such as Holm Oak (p. 128). Holly forms a shrub with leafy branches right down to ground level (since grazing animals understandably avoid it) or a tree (**5**) occasionally as high as 20m. It has smooth grey bark (**1**) and is completely evergreen. The flowers (**3**) are small, 7–8mm across, male and female on separate trees; they are white and fragrant in May but may occur during the summer. The round berries (**6**) are prominent, though green, as early as July, and redden in September to the familiar berry. In mild winters they may survive the depredations of thrushes and other birds through to March. A native of western Europe, common in lowland areas, but occurring throughout Britain except for the far north, Holly is a typical hedgerow tree and may form an understorey in oak, and especially beech, woods. Often planted for ornament or shelter, sometimes as variegated varieties.

1

SPINDLE-TREE   *Euonymus europaeus*

Though able to grow into a small tree up to about 6m tall, Spindle-tree is most often found in scrub on calcareous soil, often with privet. It rarely has a single trunk, but the main stems have grey-green bark. The twigs (**1**) have four angles and are smooth and hairless, bearing opposite pairs of narrow oval, pointed, bright green leaves (**2**). In May the small greenish-white flowers (**3**) appear, with 4 narrow, widely-spaced petals, in clusters of 3–8. The extraordinary fruits (**4**) are conspicuous in late September and October, the seeds being covered by a bright orange fleshy structure (the 'aril') and enclosed in a cherry-pink capsule: the combination is unmistakable. Widespread in Europe north of the Mediterranean as far as southern Scotland and Sweden, Spindle-tree is quite common on chalk and limestone in lowland Britain. The name derives from the use of its wood for spindles in the spinning of wool.

Broad-leaved Spindle-tree *E. latifolius* has longer and much broader leaves (**6**), 4–12 flowered clusters of 5-petalled flowers, and a larger fruit capsule (**5**) up to 2cm across. Native in central Europe and frequently planted elsewhere.

1

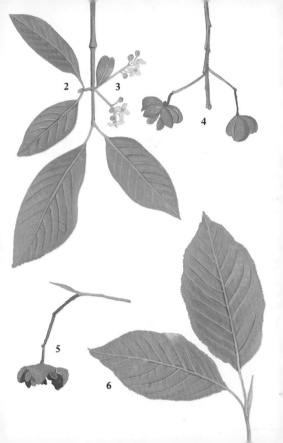

BOX *Buxus sempervirens*

Box is such a familiar garden hedging plant (**5**), the dwarf cultivar often being trimmed to within a few inches of the ground, that it comes as a surprise to find it forms a respectable small tree from 6–10m high, if left to itself. In tree form (**4**) it has one or a few slightly twisted trunks with brown, cracked bark. The glossy dark evergreen leaves (**1**) are borne in opposite pairs on the square stems and usually have their edges rolled under. The yellowish flowers (**2**) are easily missed in April, tucked away among the leaves; the clusters contain both male and female flowers, but neither has petals. The small, dry capsule (**3**) has three short prongs, but only matures in a good summer in Britain. As a native it occurs scattered throughout western Europe, and in Britain only in a few isolated localities on chalk in southern England, the best known of which is Box Hill in Surrey. It is also very commonly planted as a hedge or thicket, sometimes as pheasant cover.

Box Hill

BUCKTHORN *Rhamnus catharticus*

Buckthorn is a large bush, usually about 5m tall, which sometimes can grow into a small tree up to 10m high. Even then it usually has a well-branched trunk, with dark, rather orange-brown, scaly bark (1). Branches are produced in opposite pairs almost at right-angles to the main shoot (2), but some only develop as short shoots bearing leaves, or even as rather blunt spines. The leaf buds have dark scales; oval leaves (3) have long stalks and 2–4 pairs of spreading veins; in autumn they turn brownish yellow, in contrast to the superficially similar Alder Buckthorn (p. 208). The small 4-petalled flowers are only 4–5mm across and yellowish-green, and are produced in inconspicuous groups well back from the tips of the branches in May; male (5) and female (6) are separate. The berries (4) are glossy black in late September and October; they are poisonous with a powerful purgative (hence *catharticus*) effect. Buckthorn is a common shrub on a wide range of soils from dry chalk to fen peat, mainly in lowland England. It is found throughout Europe from the Alps to southern Scandinavia.

1

ALDER BUCKTHORN
Frangula alnus

Alder Buckthorn is sometimes confused with Buckthorn (p. 206) but rarely grows larger than 4 or 5m and forms only a bushy small tree (5) with smooth, finely cracked bark (1). It has no thorns and the branches are not quite opposite each other and make a narrow angle with the main stem; leaf buds (2) have no scales. The yellowish-green leaves (3) have 7–8 pairs of veins and turn a bright yellow in autumn. The tiny greenish-white flowers (4) are even smaller (3–4mm) than those of Buckthorn, and appear in small clusters at the tips of the branches. The glossy black berries (6) ripen slightly later than those of Buckthorn, maturing from green through a rich cherry-red. Alder Buckthorn occurs throughout Europe from the Mediterranean northwards, except for northern mountains and islands; it is not found at all in Scotland. In England it occurs widely but is absent from large areas. It prefers moist, peaty soils and tolerates more acid soils than Buckthorn.

1

2

3

4

5

6

SMALL-LEAVED LIME
Tilia cordata

A fine tree, reaching 25–30m with an uneven crown (**5**), billowing out irregularly. The bark (**2**) is greyish, and finely cracked, but broken by prominent bosses; sometimes ridged. The young twigs (**1**) are slightly downy but soon become smooth and hairless. The leaves (**4**) are quite small, rarely more than 7cm long, and heart-shaped, narrowing to a pointed tip, glossy dark green above and greyish and hairless beneath, with small tufts of orange-brown hairs. The characteristic and unmistakable flower clusters arise from a long leaf-like bract and are half-upright. Each cluster has 4–12 yellowish-white 5-petalled flowers (**3**). The fruits (**6**) are smooth and rounded with a short beak, and fall from the tree in a cluster, with the bract acting as a wing. Limes are among the latest of trees to flower, usually in early July. Small-leaved Lime is found throughout most of Europe, but only scattered in Britain, mainly in the Midlands, where it forms woods on deep, loamy soils. It is frequently planted.

1

2

3

4

5

6

COMMON LIME *Tilia × vulgaris*

A magnificent, tall tree (**3**) commonly reaching 25m, and in some places exceeding 40m. It is a hybrid between Small-leaved (p. 210) and Large-leaved Limes (below). It has bark (**2**) with long ridges and cracks and sprouting bosses, and massive leaves and it suckers freely. The twigs (**1**) are hairless and the leaves (**5**) larger than in Small-leaved Lime, from 6–10cm long, with tufts of whitish hairs underneath. The flower clusters (**4**) contain 5–10 flowers and dangle from the twigs, opening in July. The ripe fruits are faintly ribbed (**6**). A well-established hybrid, it reproduces largely by suckers, but its origin is unknown. It occurs naturally, though sparsely, throughout Europe, but is very commonly planted, particularly in avenues.

Large-leaved Lime *T. platyphyllos* usually has a clean, unbossed trunk and leaves (**7**) that are downy underneath and sometimes above as well. Flowers usually in threes, opening often in late June, always earlier than other limes; the fruit (**8**) is strongly ribbed. Widespread in central and southern Europe, and forming woods in steep limestone slopes in the Welsh Marches, around Bristol and in south Yorkshire, but possibly a long-established introduction; widely planted.

1

2

3

4

5

6

7

8

BLUE GUM *Eucalyptus globulus*

Gum trees are tall and very fast-growing Australasian trees with evergreen foliage, normally distinct on young and old branches. They are very widely planted in the Mediterranean for timber, shelter and amenity. Blue Gum is scarcely hardy in England but common in Ireland and further south. It is a large tree (**7**) reaching 40m, with multicoloured peeling bark (**2**) fading from oranges and pinks when new to a greyish-brown. The leaves on the young shoots (**3**) are unstalked and blue-grey, those on the old shoots (**6**) are sickle-shaped, greener and up to 30cm long. Flowers (**5**) have a curious disc-like structure with a ring of stamens; they occur individually. Blue Gum has a very large fruits (**1** and **4**) up to 3cm.

Cider Gum *E. gunnii* is one of the hardiest species and by far the most commonly planted in England and occasionally surviving in Scotland. It has rounded, blue, unstalked juvenile leaves and larger, narrower, pointed mature leaves (**8**). It flowers in July. Though quite hardy it still succumbs to severe frosts.

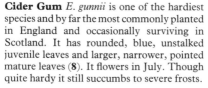

A dozen or so other *Eucalyptus* species are grown in Europe but very few are hardy.

3

4

5

6

7

8

CORNELIAN CHERRY
Cornus mas

A small tree, reaching 8–10m, with smooth bark (**2**), or a spreading, much-branched shrub (**5**). It flowers very early, in February and March, producing conspicuous tight clusters of bright yellow flowers (**3**) on the bare greyish-green twigs (**1**). Individual flowers have four tiny pointed petals, 2–3mm long, and the whole cluster sits on four yellow-green bracts that soon fall. The pointed oval leaves (**4**) have prominent veins and are borne in pairs along the twigs. The unusual lozenge-shaped fruits (**6**) are a rich bright red and give this plant its inappropriate name; they are 12–15mm long. Cornelian Cherry occurs throughout lowland central Europe in open woods and scrub, usually on chalk and limestone; it is widely planted in gardens, sometimes in a variegated form, and is occasionally naturalized in Britain.

1

2

detail of flowers

3

4

5

6

RHODODENDRON
Rhododendron ponticum

A massive spreading shrub or small tree (**4**), this is the rhododendron that is frequently encountered as an almost complete shrub layer, particularly in oak or birch woods on acid sandy or dry peaty soils. It is in fact native in southern Spain and Portugal and in south-east Europe but is so widely planted and so readily sets seed that it has become extraordinarily widely naturalized. It has large many-scaled buds, and dark green leathery leaves (**2**), paler underneath and up to 25cm long. The flowers are in dense clusters at the tips of the branches, surrounded by a ruff of leaves. They appear in June and each has the shape of a spreading bell (**3**) and is a striking pinkish-purple, up to 6cm across, and with 10 stamens. The seeds are produced in a dry capsule. The bark (**1**) is also illustrated.

1

Yellow Rhododendron *R. luteum* is smaller and deciduous, its 5-stamened yellow flowers (**5**) appearing on the leafless shoots in April and May. A rare native of central and south-east Europe, it is often grown in gardens and is occasionally naturalized.

Many other tree-forming *Rhododendron* species are planted but none are naturalized.

STRAWBERRY TREE
Arbutus unedo

In the wild, in south-west Ireland and in the Mediterranean, Strawberry Tree is normally a large spreading shrub up to 2–3m high, but in cultivation it reaches 10–12m (**4**). The dark brown bark (**1**) peels off in strips, revealing fresh red-brown flashes. It has narrow, glossy, dark green, hairless leaves (**3**) up to 10cm long and 2–3 times as long as wide. It flowers very late in the year, from late September onwards, its creamy flask-shaped flowers (**2**) produced in hanging, red-stalked clusters of 15–20. The fruit take a whole year to mature, so that at the same time the plant bears small clusters (rarely more than half a dozen survive to fruition) of bright orange-red warty footballs (**5**), which, from some fanciful resemblance to strawberries, give the plant its name; there is, of course, no relationship, the true Strawberry belonging to the Rose Family, the Strawberry Tree to the Heather Family. In the Mediterranean it grows in dry, rock scrublands, in Ireland on rocky islands in lakes, and in oak scrub. Also a common garden plant in southern England.

1

2

3

4

5

ASH *Fraxinus excelsior*

The only native tree of the Olive Family, Ash forms a rather untidy, crown (**8**), often with prominent dead branches, 20–25m high – exceptionally 40m. The trunk is often long and straight and the initially smooth grey bark becomes split by long ridges and fissures on older trees (**2**). The twigs (**5**) give ash-woods a grey glow in winter, and bear distinctive large black buds (**4**). The leaves (**7**) are pinnate with 3–7 pairs of leaflets each up to 10cm long. It is one of the last native trees to come into leaf, and the leaves usually fall when still green. The flowers (**6**) may be male, female or hermaphrodite, as may whole trees; they appear in April before the leaves and, if male, are dark purple. The fruits (**1**) are shed in October, and each is set in a long narrow brown wing, notched at the tip – the samaras or 'keys'. An important woodland tree, Ash forms pure stands on limestones and in upland areas. In northern England it is the main hedgerow tree. Widespread in Europe.

Manna or Flowering Ash *F. ornus* is a smaller tree with smooth bark (**3**), grey-brown buds, smaller leaves (**9**) and prominent white flowers (**10**). Native of the Mediterranean widely planted.

4

5

6

7

8

9

10

OLIVE *Olea europaea*

A grove of olives is the quintessential Mediterranean view, immortalized by Van Gogh. Olive is in fact a native tree of the Mediterranean, and the cultivated variety has larger leaves and fruits. It is a squat tree (**6**) reaching 15m, with a massive, often contorted, trunk and grey, fissured bark (**1**). Cultivated plants have narrow greyish leaves (**2**) but the wild variety has rounded leaves and spiny twigs. The flowers are produced in short spikes (**3**) arising from the base of the leaves, each very small, with four whitish petals. They mature to give the familiar fruits (**4**) green at first and finally black (**5**), from which the economically important oil is pressed. Wild trees occur in scrub in dry rocky places, and groves of cultivated olives are found all over the Mediterranean.

1

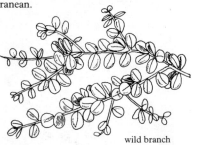

wild branch

FOXGLOVE TREE   *Paulownia tomentosa*

Foxglove Tree derives its name more from its membership of the same botanical family as foxglove than from the rather forced similarity between their flowers. It is a medium-sized tree (**4**), usually 10–15m high, but occasionally more, with an open crown and smooth grey bark. The leaves (**2**, much reduced, and **3**) are heart-shaped with a long, tapering point, 30–35cm long, and downy on both sides. This gives them a dull green colour and combined with their tendency to hang limply from the branches lends the tree a somewhat weary appearance. Some leaves may be larger and lobed. The large (5cm long) flowers (**1**) are violet-blue and have deep tubes and five spreading lobes. They appear in June before the leaves in tall irregular spikes. Fruits (**5**) are pale green, oblong, and tough, with a small, pointed beak, eventually splitting when brown to release the winged seeds. A Chinese tree widely planted in southern Europe and less often north to southern England.

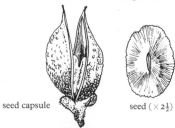

seed capsule   seed ($\times 2\frac{1}{2}$)

1

2   3

4

5

INDIAN BEAN TREE
Catalpa bignonioides

The Indians referred to here are American, for this is an introduced species from the southern United States, and despite its frost-tenderness, much favoured for planting in southern England. In general appearance it resembles a greener version of Foxglove Tree (p. 226), but it comes into leaf very late – in late June – and has white flowers, giving it something of the appearance of a small Horse Chestnut (**6**). It has ridged, scaly bark (**2**), fat twigs with prominent leaf scars (**1**) and leaves (**4**) with a rounded base or slightly heart-shaped. Both flower spike and flowers (**5**) are similar in shape to Foxglove Tree, but are white, and open in July. The extraordinary seed pods (**3**) are perhaps its most distinctive feature and give the plant its name. They are up to 40cm long and hang from the branches through the winter. Commonly planted in southern Europe and occasionally natural-ized.

1

2

seed

ELDER *Sambucus nigra*

A familiar shrub or small tree (**7**), reaching 10m exceptionally, Elder behaves more like a weed than a tree, springing up with astonishing speed on disturbed ground and in cracks in concrete paths and similar places. The bark (**3**) on mature trunks is brown and deeply furrowed, that on younger branches is smooth with well-marked pores (lenticels) (**1**). If a twig is broken the wood is very soft and pithy (**2**). It has pinnate leaves (**6**) with, usually, 2–3 pairs of leaflets which vary from rounded to narrow oval, and occasionally may be deeply toothed. The flowers are minute, about 5mm across, but are prominent in profuse, flat-topped clusters (**4**), 10–20cm across, appearing in June and smelling of cats. The fruits (**5**) are ripe in late August and September, the familiar black elderberries, edible and striking on their red stalks. The flower clusters stand upright in flower but bend down with the weight of the fruit. Common throughout Europe except the far north, usually on disturbed soils and, since its leaves are unpleasant-tasting, it grows well around rabbit burrows.

Red-berried Elder *S. racemosa* has a rounded flowerhead and red berries (**8**). Central Europe and Scandinavia; naturalized in Scotland.

DATE PALM *Phoenix dactylifera*

Palms are quite unmistakable: being mono-
cotyledons (like grasses, sedges and lilies)
their stems are not woody but fibrous and
continually grow giving a cluster of leaves
perched as much as 20m from the ground (**2**).
The trunk is largely made up of the old leaf
bases which remain in a series of conspicuous
spirals on the trunk (**1**). The leaves are huge,
several metres long, with many pairs of long,
narrow, greyish leaflets. The flowers are
borne in massive dangling clusters (**3**) arising
from the top of the trunk. The immature
green fruits (**4**) are all that is usually seen in
Europe; to ripen into the familiar date (**5**) they
need a true hot desert climate. Nevertheless
Date Palms are widely planted for ornament
throughout the Mediterranean.

Canary Palm *P. canariensis* is a smaller tree
(**6**) up to 10m, with a fat trunk, bright green
leaves and dry fruits. A native of the Canaries,
it is often planted in the Mediterranean.

1

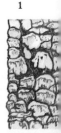

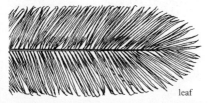

leaf

Index of English Names

Index of Scientific Names